TANGO CONFIDENTIAL

A memoir from the dance floor

MARCY GOLDMAN

MONTREAL, CANADA

Tango Confidential

A memoir from the dance floor

Original Text and Poetry by Marcy Goldman

River Heart Press 2023

Montreal, Canada

Library and Archives Canada in Publication

ISBN 978-1-927936-44-3 Print Book

ISBN 978-1-927936-43-6 E-book

Other Books by Marcy Goldman, all available in print and e-book

The Baker's Dozen Volume Three Best Bagels, River Heart Press 2021

The Baker's Dozen Volume Four Best Scones, River Heart Press 2021

The Baker's Dozen Volume Two Best Biscotti, River Heart Press 2017

The Baker's Dozen Volume One Best Holiday Cookies, River Heart Press 2016

The 10th Anniversary Edition Jewish Holiday Baking, River Heart Press 2017

The New Best of Betterbaking.com, River Heart Press 2017

The Newish Jewish Cookbook, River Heart Press 2019

A Passion for Baking, River Heart Press 2014

The Baker's Four Seasons River Heart Press 2014

Love and Ordinary Things River Heart Press 2014

When Bakers Cook, River Heart Press 2013

A Treasury of Jewish Holiday Baking Whitecap Books 2007

The New Best of Betterbaking.com Whitecap Books 2007

Marcy Goldman is a professional pastry chef and cookbook author. She's been dancing since she's five years old and dancing tango specifically for a long time with no plans to stop anytime soon. She may be reached via her website www.betterbaking.com.

DEDICATION

To the hosts of the diverse Montreal tango community and the places where I first learned to dance and still frequent. To the dedicated teachers both here and those who have visited from around the globe, the DJ's and the musicians and all the s upport people who make tango in Montreal happen every single day of the week

To my fellow *tangueros* world-wide who understand the passion

To Argentina for sharing the love

To my friends and also my readers at Betterbaking.com who read my tango tales in my baking newsletters and never found mixing flour and butter with tango steps a strange recipe

And lastly, mostly,

To my three sons who I love infinitely more than tango

To be fond of dancing was a certain
step towards falling in love.

Jane Austen, Pride and Prejudice

We dance to seduce ourselves, to fall in love with
ourselves. When we dance with another we manifest
the very thing we love about ourselves so that they
may see it and love us too.

Kamand Kojouri

When a body moves, it's the most revealing thing.
Dance for a minute, and I'll tell you who you are.

Mikhail Baryshnikov

TABLE OF CONTENTS

THE DANCE BEGINS

INTRODUCTION

Several years ago, a few days after I left my twenty-two year marriage, I was feeling utterly rudderless and lost but I also wasn't alone. I had three young, bewildered sons whose lives I had just upended also along for the ride.

I was in my kitchen one morning after the school buses had left, getting ready to ruminate about my broken-apart life when I saw a newspaper ad for Argentine Tango.

It was a hot, dry, late August day, one that was thickly laced with the dusty fragrance of summer-on-its-way out. The air and atmosphere felt tense, motionless and dull. In that raw, initial week of being newly-single, I swung between intense moods of anxiety, sadness and relief. Although I was sitting among the entrails of a failed marriage at least I had done the hard part which was leaving altogether. But everything else aside from pivotal decision winnowed down to just one thing: an overwhelming craving to be held.

The local newspaper tango class ad was sketchy at best; it featured a silhouette of a couple dancing with a banner over them saying: *Free Introduction Tango Class* but it immediately triggered something in me. I was dancer since I was five years old. That side of me included ballet, modern, jazz, and stints in musical theatre. For me, dance had always been a constant. Through all of life's ups and downs, dance had fed, sustained and centered me. Now gazing at that free dance class ad I suddenly decided it was time to both end the dancing hiatus and inaugurate my second-act life by trying something new but innately familiar. The idea of couple dancing naturally had disproportionate appeal. *I can go back to dance and that might help,* I told myself. I concurrently thought, albeit less audibly even in the quiet place in my own head: *perhaps I'll meet someone there.*

That was a Friday afternoon. On the following Monday night I found my way to that free introductory class. The tango studio was in a different part of town – as far from the suburbs geographically and philosophically as it could possibly be. I crammed myself into an electric blue leotard from amateur theater days, grabbed an old pair of black character shoes and hopped out the door. As I left I flung a pizza at my three sons and the babysitter, one of the few brave teenage souls willing to manage three wild boys. I waved goodbye and goodnight in one breathless motion.

When I arrived at the vintage ballroom that served as the tango studio I inhaled the heavy wafts of sangria, saffron and *Gitanos* from the Spanish restaurant downstairs. Clearly I wasn't in Kansas anymore. I opened the door and tentatively made my way inside and in a flash I tumbled down the tango rabbit hole, truly a portal to another world. Since then I've never looked back and so many years later I'm still tumbling.

As a writer and avid journal-keeper it was natural to me to start a blog called *Tango Confidential* which was a staging area for my vignettes about my tango life. The blog kept me inspired as I wrote about tango, still fresh in my mind from tango evenings and weekend classes. Almost as much as tango itself, the writing *about* tango kept up my spirits up as a single mother to three sons, trying to balance parenting, work and life. I maintained my other, daily bread writing life as a professional baker, cookbook author and host of my website, www.betterbaking.com. Via my monthly baking newsletter, *A Note from Marcy,* I probably babbled about tango too often for the comfort of my readers, sharing my tango escapades between the cookie, cake and scone recipes. I always found some metaphor about life, baking and tango to share. But there's a limit to how much tango chatter you can squeeze in-between biscuits and bread and I knew one day I would honor my tango experiences by giving them a home in a book of their own.

This book is comprised of vignettes that are unique moments in my tango life. I've still tried to create somewhat of a timeline arc of how tango unfolded for me as a neophyte dancer to the full-fledged *tanguera* I hope I now am. So much of tango is not just about the dance steps but learning the social codes that go with it.

I've divided the book into traditional chapters but also companion *Interludes* which are shorter observations and experiences that are an integral part of my whole tango life. The poetry in the book (as well as a couple of recipes) are all my original works.

As we emerge from the darkest days of the pandemic, tango has taken on even more allure, drawing back veteran dancers as well as a whole slew of newcomers. As I've made my own return to classes ranked with both masked and unmasked dancers, all I can feel is the sheer joy of being back! There's far more diverse people than ever before who have joined this special world, as well as other dance venues, presumably all in response to life lightening up. There seems to be a reactive hunger collectively felt of *real* people wanting to connect with other, *real* people in real time.

During the initial pandemic lockdown and the subsequent closing (forever or for three years) of the tango places I usually went to, I've done my fair share of virtual tango. I've danced with a broomstick as my partner on *Zoom,* taking lessons with others around the world, similarly isolated in the lock-down and hungry to continue dancing and needing to connect. That worked well enough for a time throughout the enforced tango hiatus but nothing compares to being back with actual, live people.

Tango Confidential is a memoir of my life on the dance floor and it's a journey that continues. What I share is unique as all tango experiences are because the journey for each of us is as individual as our fingerprints and or dance steps. Many books speak of the pedagogy of tango, about its history or its music and many others are memoirs of a newly enthralled tango dancer who travels to Buenos Aires in a soul-searching mid-life romantic escape. But what I have discovered at the tango is something that has been powerful and life-altering. It's changed the way I see the world outside tango as well as inside it. To a greater or lesser extent, it's that way for almost everyone I've ever met; once you try it, you're never the same. I sometimes say tango is once or terminal since few people ever leave its fold. They may take a break at times but they always return.

In this modern life that we all click away in, there's an undeclared disconnection that runs like subtle, default background software in our human selves. World events, global viruses and digital-socio evolutions only seem to accentuate it. Sometimes I think the clicking of our devices is more of an echo of a ticking clock of loneliness that won't abate. Thankfully there is a legal and accessible cure for this disconnect. It's called *Argentine Tango* and it has the power to exorcise the disconnect, send the isolation packing and glue you back to your center. At the same time, it can tether you to others in a very meaningful and impactful way that almost nothing else, at least for me, ever has. Tango is something that definitely needs to be shared because it's too good to covet. Is tango it romantic? Absolutely! But's it's also so much more because like the best of authentic romances, tango is one that renews its vows over and over again.

You can reside in this special place if only for a few hours, repairing what's hurt or finding what's been lost. This is a winged world where your soul finds its way home and your spirit takes flight. There's no net and you never touch ground.

If you've always dreamed of tango but were too cautious to go, please accept this book is your invitation to explore it from the safety of your day-to-day life. I'm delighted to unveil the secrets from dance floor. Let me be your guide to a sweet demi-monde that is purring away even as you nod off, fretting over taxes, unwashed laundry and unanswered emails. I have the shoes, the dress and the attitude. I know the best places and where to match the mood to the venue. I'll take care of all these things if you just let me lead. The rest of the world is sleeping as tango is just waking up. But to quote Rumi, *don't go back to sleep*. Come with me instead.

Tango begins with one simple phrase that's the same no matter what language you speak. Aside from *I love you* the most beautiful three words I know are simply and always: *shall we dance?*

Please say yes.

Marcy Goldman
Montreal, Canada

PROLOGUE
BEFORE THE FIRST TANGO

No se como hice para hacer eso...
Con la respiración me salió.

I don't know how I did it... but with
the breathing, it happened.
Alberto Podesta

Music cue: Tango entr'acte music, soft bandoneon, something Nuevo, perhaps Astor Pizzazolla but something sad and quietly insistent like an embrace that won't quit.

There's a woman alone in her kitchen who is very familiar. I know her for she is in fact, me. I observe myself as I am being myself, sort of like those big paintings you stare at until you wonder about actually *being* in the painting. First you wander with your eyes and then with your mood until you're actually inside the painting yourself and then it all blurs and you know longer know what is real and what is a projection.

In the background there are the faint echoes of children who live there but who aren't at home. This is a quiet, empty house on a late August day and I'm dwelling on unanswerable questions. This breeds a disquiet that makes me feel untethered and spacey. Is a mother still a mother when the rest of the cast is out?

I don't wait to ponder an answer because suddenly I'm in the pantry and the fridge. There's a slight rustle of opening and closing packages, cans, a twist of a jar of peanut butter – a minor symphony of sounds all related to food. What to eat, what to snack on, what to gnaw on? I paw at sweet and salty, crunchy, soft, and all manner of chewy possibilities until I catch myself. I just stop and stay as still as a guilty statue. Even that takes huge resistance because everything is shaking inside. My very bones feel like rattling plates and fragile China cups all clattering away but I force myself to stay in place. I listen to the hum of the air conditioner for five, maybe eight full seconds. I glance at the phone messages on the fridge that say: *call mediator/call notary/call back locksmith.* Should I call the divorce lawyer and see if anything new has eventuated requiring some response? Should I wash the outside of the fridge where I notice there's tiers of fingermarks and streaks of melted chocolate? Instead I lean against back the cool stainless fridge door and try to reckon with whatever it is I want to avoid feeling.

A fresh separation feels like an ache that will only heal after it's allowed to feel itself for a while. As a professional baker I know there's no way to rush to resolutions. You can neither hurry bread or pain. But I can't seem to fully name or locate the ache; it travels from the heart to the bones and resonates there in the marrow where I can neither reach nor soothe. I walk over to the dining-room table and open the newspaper and a small ad catches my eye:

Introduction to Basic Tango
Free Tango Lesson - beginners, couples and singles.
Tuesday, 7-9, Spanish Social Club

I try and concentrate on the ad but that unmoored feeling returns and the rumination it triggers begins all over again.

You would think the book being done would have done *something* for it is *finally* done and yet I'm definitely feeling edgy and I'm confounded by the lack of relief in having finished the book. I throw out the morning coffee in lieu of knowing what else to do but also because I hate cold coffee. It reminds me of when the boys were toddlers and I never got to finish a single cup of hot, fresh brew. As a consequence I've never like iced coffees no matter how gourmet or upscale they seem regardless of how they tout it. It's simply ice-cold, left-standing, unfinished coffee totally bereft of the warmth of its original intended comfort.

So I make a new cup with that Brazilian blend that was obscenely expensive but at the time of purchase I said, *never mind, I deserve it and when the book is done, I'm treating myself.* I observe the coffee as it drips down into a vintage white Pier I mug which has just the right heft to its handle, perfectly housing 12 ounces of coffee. I sip and wait for the feeling of (ironic) calm from caffeine. When none comes, I find myself nibbling on leftover toast and silently admonish myself because I had breakfast but an hour ago. But it is such *good* toast; I bake it myself from a lovingly cared-for sourdough starter. The bread that comes from it is my own special recipe although everyone knows sourdough is all technique – the recipe is so *not* the point. The sourdough munch begins another debate: good carbs versus bad carbs. I really dislike the nutritionists! Even the wellness industry is a cover up for the diet industry. I finish the bread crust and debate creating a gluten-free version of the recipe which is hardly my beat as a classically-trained baker but I figure I can pitch it to *Epicurious* or *Costco* or stick it in whatever cookbook I'm working on.

I move on from the toast and start a game of tag with a jar of *Nutella. Just a taste, a spoon*, I tell the impassive face of the kitchen clock, *no more than that.* The calorie count on the back of the jar is conveniently smudged with chocolate so I can't read it. Just as well. What is it? 735 calories per level tablespoon? 59% calories from fat? *Nutella* is definitely pantry *Prozac*. And now I am back on the nervous nibbling, all over again.

By now I'm pacing and my mind is amuck with culinary trivia. I debate making homemade French croissants again for the first time. *I could do an article on that.* I idly consider making out-of-season marmalade with seedless clementines and impressing everyone. "*Yes, she actually invented that, with clementines no less, a whole new marmalade. You can't buy stuff like that*"

I'm not even a fan of marmalade. It always looks so pretty but tastes so bittersweet. It's not even nicely bittersweet in that charming literary sort of way of bittersweet but off-putting/bittersweet in the-you-wince-when-you-taste-it sort of way. Maybe it is the Finishing the Book thing. Everyone was so relieved. "*How's that book coming along?*" "*What's with that book of yours*"? The Book - that unending, unfinished, terminally incomplete-work-in-progress book.

How's the book is sort of like "*how's your mom*?" and '*how are the kids*?" No one really expects to hear something new nor do they listen to whatever it is you answer. But I did it! I did finish it finally and so now when people asked, '*how's the book*?" I could say, "*Done*". The funny thing is that they seemed almost disappointed when I said it was completed.

I clean the kitchen pantry, re-line a drawer with scented *Crabtree and Evelyn* paper and then take out some old poems to read again and debate if I should self-publish them. As a matter of fact, one of them got published in the New York Times – more than one, two or three or so in *Metropolitan Diary.*

The Late News

One night,
Just before bed
But just after the news
He caught her staring into space
"Hey" he said,
"What's wrong?"
Nothing.
"Nothing?"
No.
But her eyes glistened
A touch too bright
But then again,
It could just have been the light.

As I'm reading, the phone rings. Turns out it's some broadcaster, a local AM lifestyle radio personality asking if I'd come into the station to be interviewed. "*We have a show here for local goings-on. We can talk about whatever-it-is-you-I-hear-you-wrote a cookbook?*" Clearly his producer has told him to follow up on something, i.e. my new cookbook that he hardly cares about but it's part of his job of covering local stories. I listen with half an ear his perfunctory tone and wonder if he can possible perceive how distant his voice sounds to me and how much less his call means to *me* than it means to him. But I say *yes* anyway, trying to feel grateful for the outreach.

I thank him for asking me and hang up.

I glance back at a box of *Wheat Thins* for a minute and then gaze back at the Free Tango Class ad. I dial the number.

As the number rings, I glance at the pantry but just as my eyes return to the siren's lure of that damned cracker box I get a recorded message. *Class starts next week. Please leave your number.* I carefully say my cell phone number out loud and I leave my name afterwards. I may have left my phone number twice, stating it again at the end of my message for good measure. I don't think for one moment that I will be learning how to dance. Instead I think: *someone will finally hold me.*

I call the divorce lawyer and leave a message. Then I call the locksmith and make an appointment for the next day. I check in with my thoughts and notice that for the time-being, the haunt of constant rumination has ceased. I can actually hear the quiet of the house now that the inner chatter has stopped.

I forget the *Wheat Thins*, the *Nutella*, the clementine marmalade and the cold coffee.

Instead I try and breathe but all I can do is take in big gulps of shallow breaths that leave me even more breathless until I realize I'm actually panting. I force myself to slow down and after several attempts more temperate breathing takes hold. As the minutes pass and I feel my mind and feelings settle back into body I begin to accept that's there no escape. Breathe and breathe again. But I want *more* than air, *more* than oxygen, *more* than what is around me. I want escape from whatever it is that's chasing me from the inside. But there's no safe place or higher ground and I vaguely realize the only way *out* it is *through* it. The only option is to be uncomfortable and stay exactly where I am. So I start slowly once again, in and out, breath by breath, like hesitant steps moving forward made with shallow exhalations. I take one larger breath and just stay still, holding my breath until I can't anymore and finally I allow myself to breathe out, loud, long and clear.

And then I just breathe as if things are ordinary or at least somewhat ok and like I am a normal person. In and out, in and out. At some point I'm no longer aware of my breath - mercifully it has become organic. And at the same time, I notice I no longer feel hungry.

CHAPTER ONE

TANGO FOR BEGINNERS

I really don't know what I'm doing here. I *could* have stayed home and watched *Angels in the Outfield* with the boys for the tenth time which granted isn't exciting but definitely more comfortable. At least I know what's expected of me there: make the popcorn. But I can't continue to do what I *always* do because I've essentially toppled over into a new life that I don't properly fit quite the same way as I did in my old life. To be fair, I didn't fit that life either insofar as how it was constructed and the various players in it but at least I knew my place. Yet here I am. I'm still a mother of three young sons and Have Responsibilities. I also have to work and have work which is seemingly more and more of a career that I have to pay attention to and more to the point, it's what is keeping us all fed, housed and clothed. It's essentially all on me. Ironically, the thing I wanted *not to be* is *exactly* what I have become: divorced and also, coincidentally a working writer. It should be understood being a writer, even a working one, isn't the sort of endeavour one should even consider if regular groceries have an appeal or if you're a single parent of just one child let alone a trio. Writing as your day job is what you do if you married well and/or teach three hours a week at some university for an exorbitant amount of revenue and job security. I'm not in either of those categories and suffice to say there's a real urgency to my art.

My life is a vortex of pitching agents, publishers and editors alongside car pools of other people's kids (and one or two of my own), sorting socks, cleaning lunch packs and being late for everything that I should be early for or at the very least on time if in fact I remember where I have to be or what I have to do altogether. I'm one colossal come-up-short experiment. My life is the additive inverse of what I imagined and had mapped out. Speaking of maps, there is none. I will have to make this up as I go along.

A dormant part of me, that unexplored, single adult part that got consummately supplanted by another version now wants out. *That* version worked until it didn't and now it's waking up full of uncertainty and intention which is to say, I'm navigating by an uneasy, undirected energy. It has an innate hunger attached to it and it's one that insists I go and find all the life that is made up of the choices *not* taken when one opts for door #1 (married, suburbs, children) until one chooses door #2 (no longer married, keep the suburbs, keep the children). I'm starved to see other adults *not* involved in bantam hockey and baseball try-outs and car pools plus I miss music and dance in my life. Those things want feeding.

The piece of paper saying *Free Tango Class* torn from the newspaper sits crumpled up on the passenger car seat. At home the ad looked crisp and exciting (oh how renegade I am!) and now it's both a mopey reproach and a subtle challenge. I'm very tempted to back down and in some circles I'm even known as the Queen of the Bail. And truth is, I *can* back down because honestly, who would know? I didn't tell anyone where I was going tonight although of course the babysitter has my cell number. No one can fathom why I left my marriage in the first place let alone why I'm off to a tango class. But *I* would know if I reneged. In what has been a patch of time that is chock full of defeats both large and trivial, I need the win of even a small act of courage. Besides which if my revolt is not a free tango class I'll end up buying a cat and an excess of wind chimes and it's far too early days for that.

I can't believe my reconnaissance has directed me to pull up to this place. Outside this semi-historic looking building it *says Español Centro* or in English, it's the *Social Spanish Cultural Club.* The art deco building befits the name, that's for sure. What's also certain is that it doesn't look at all like the suburban landscape I've been used to for the twelve years of married-with-children life. I can feel myself stretching with discomfort like a cat that wants to retrace its steps backwards. As I go inside there's not much on the first floor but I do notice the sign saying *Tango Class* with a crooked arrow pointing upward. I start up the stairs, clutching a make-shift black dance bag with some character shoes from my amateur theatre days. I'm wearing a black skirt and electric blue leotard with a modest ballet neckline that I chose, reasoning that in just case I look like I'm in a costume I might get away with wearing something that's not too different from normal street clothes. More pointedly, I didn't know what to wear and frankly nothing fit. Already I feel like an imposter, squished into the blue dance wear, having worn nothing but baggy Lululemon and Old Navy athletic wear for over a decade which suits my day life but clearly has no place here.

On the way up I pass by a dark iron-gated bar or restaurant. There's a sprawl of middle-aged men inside, smoking cigars and unfiltered cigarettes. I hear the tinkling of wine glasses and notice a large punch bowl of what seem to be sangria but my overall take-away is a sea of dark moustaches heavily into conversations both lively and serious. I half expect Eva Perón to stroll by. Clearly the tango studio has interesting neighbours. A light scent of saffron and olive oil follows me as I go up the stairs along with a few long stares that register abject disinterest before the stares and their moustached owners return to the conversations at hand.

I find the doors to the class and timidly open them, trying to be quiet and unobtrusive only to realize I have to give it a big hoist to get it open and am rewarded with a huge high-pitched creaking sound which announces my arrival in the most conspicuous way possible. I want to shrink, turn around and flee but there in front of me is a beautiful vintage ballroom. It smells musty and moldy but not too terribly. There's a magnificent stage and acres of amber-hued, heavily patina-ed wood dance floor. About twelve to fifteen people are milling around in a semi-circle and I think, *well, there's still time to escape* and I turn quickly and almost manage to bolt but one of the teachers gets to the door before me. She briskly closes it and then ushers me closer into the center room with a friendly sweep of her arm around my back. There's no escape. *Hola, welcome to tango.*

Inwardly I curse myself for choosing adventure over sameness considering all else in my life had been shaken to the foundation. I hardly need another hoop to jump or a test with anything remotely exotic. But here I am and at the least this presents a great occasion to practise poise. If it's any consolation, I notice that everyone else also looks uncomfortable. If I was less self-absorbed and innately less self-conscious I might be curious about what brought them here.

I try and listen to the instructions which are mostly in French which I understand and speak but that calls for more concentration and interferes with my people-observing-and-assessing. My thoughts also flit to the boys who must have tied up the sitter by now. I pray the house is still standing when I return.

At first, all we do at first is walk around the ballroom, strolling like people in the park on a Sunday afternoon that brings George Seurat's paintings to mind. Easy enough; I can do this. But just as we get comfortable strolling with a stranger, the main event intervenes.

Now we're asked to partner up, link arms and this time stroll with one person leading and one person following, so to speak. We stop and start as per the body language of the lead stroller. Then we break apart and create the large circle again. I glance at my watch and see only twenty minutes has gone by. For sure my house has caught fire by this point or perhaps there is an undetected sink hole which will reveal itself tonight while I was off dancing.

Next the two teachers tell everyone to choose a partner and I have that fleeting panic that's a mash-up of not being chosen for basketball and musical chairs. What if no one chooses me and there's no chair left? Do you *ever* graduate the high school of life? Odd couples are forming and thankfully, *just* as I thought I would melt in discomfort a bespeckled guy, a few years younger than me, purposely strides over to me and asks me to partner him. Thank goodness! Now that I was picked there's one less thing to worry about. I haven't been picked in over two decades and I like his confidence. His assertiveness in turn makes me feel more definite about myself.

Then we practise the simple steps of walking in partners and then, blessedly *finally,* music is put on and the first strains of classic *Tango Argentine* music *breathes* and weaves its way. Walking becomes (somewhat) dancing.

The sixty minutes passed like a dream! My feet might have hurt – they probably do - but I forgot to notice. I even forgot who I was and where I was. I only seem to exist in that single hour between coming here and not-yet-leaving. The feeling I have is that I have finally felt alive for the first time in ages. I feel almost happy or almost like 'old' me, the one that was happy before I became that morose, default stranger who supplanted me.

I barely remember signing up for a series of twelve classes but evidently I did and was simultaneously reassured there would be a partner for me. *Not to worry,* said the teacher.

I don't remember the walk back down the stairs and getting into my car. It's like when you fall in love so instantly that all else becomes a dream state. At last, I was getting back into dance, instantly captive to this totally strange dance called tango. Once home, I paid the babysitter and checked on the boys – all quiet on the western front. Miraculously everything at home base looked the same as when I left it three hours prior but everything inside me had shifted.

Now: how to last until a next week until the next tango class! How to contain my smiles and joy and how to explain it to anyone? There are no words and who am I going to tell? I'm already a cautionary tale.

I fall asleep, browsing tango shoes online, still in that silly old black dance skirt and vintage leotard. When I wake up around six am, to make the boys' lunches, I realize I slept like a lamb for the first time in months. I feel refreshed and lighter. For a moment, I forget all my usual worries and problems and don't, for at least a second, even remember what day it is. Evidentally it must be Tuesday because one of the boys tapped on my door:

Mom – it's early band practise; we have to go!

Right.

And just like that I am back in Kansas.

TANGO LESSONS

Do you know
How to tango?
C'est facile -

You place your hand
Gently on my back
And it's
Step, glide, glide
If you will lead
I will follow
And gently bring you back
Dance is just
A matter of trust
A simple exercise
In parry and thrust.
Can you tango?
Will you tango with me?

CHAPTER TWO

TINY DANCER WAKES UP

It's barely been three months and yet I sense tango is changing me in so many ways both obvious and subtle. It's waking up my inner dancer, launched when I was five – the little girl who went to Saturday morning ballet classes long before the little girls that followed segued into soccer and hockey. In those days, so many of us went to ballet school, pink leather shoes in hand, barre work, conformity and Chopin piano for our warm-ups. Somehow I kept that little dancer awake for a long time afterwards by taking drop-in dance classes in modern and jazz dance until I had my second son. At that point, life got too complicated. Along with my thread-bare Raggedy Anne doll and Magic Eight Ball and other artifacts of childhood, I had to stuff the dancer in me deep down and hidden away. In quick time, real life moved in and squashed down almost everything that was essentially me or the 'me' I knew and loved best. That person had to vacate the premises as it was just too hard to keep both versions going. But with tango, that impish dancing spirit is pummeling on the gates, itching to get out and strut her stuff. That's the thing when you leave hungry things unfed and alone too long; they revolt and want to make up for lost time in a way that's too fierce to ignore.

I'm embarrassed to admit that I've become that meme of a mid-life crisis dancer. All those movies: *Shall We Dance* (both the original Japanese and the American versions), *Strictly Ballroom, A Chorus Line* are true! Some of us just gotta dance and *if* and *when* we forget that dancing hunger or whatever creative, expressive beast lives in us it returns with a vengeance.

Lately I dance in the neighbourhood streets around sundown and in my own driveway. I also dance big: not little subtle, half-extended steps but full-out grand jetés, arabesques, tango ouchos, salsa and ballroom style waltz with exaggerated Disney princess styling. I even do this in public albeit usually no one is around but I'm not sure I would care anyway.

I dance in my seat in the car, doing car pool drop-offs or waiting at stop lights. The other day I danced in the ballroom dance shoe store, trying on black fancy dance heels with a gorgeous red suede trim, just *thinking* about the *next* time I will get to dance. I've danced in an empty aisle of Costco, the weight room at the gym and in the parks on the baseball diamonds and behind the bleacher seats. I've danced in the waiting room at my endocrinologist. Recently I installed a ballet barre in my bedroom and been sewing pink satin ribbons on pink kid ballet shoes and giving them a spin to the music of *Lord of the Dance.* I do pliés watching *Good Morning America.* Last week I bumped into a guy from tango at

Staples where I was printing out my cookbook manuscript. We ended up dancing some steps near the photo-copier, oblivious to the rest of the store and customers, just to go over from step from class. I'm a veritable trope or at the least part of a montage in a mature rom-com wherein the character is in that happy, upward spiral. Watching that film you can point out and say: *there, that's when she began to change.*

Admittedly all this motion is not due exclusively to tango. It was first ignited in Miss Elsie Solomon's Dance Class when I was a child. The other girls went to after-school ballet which I also did briefly. But early on it was evident I'd never could get the conformity thing down which to me, seemed to be what early ballet was about. In addition it was also about the discipline and beautiful techniques which thankfully I did pick up. At that young age I wasn't ready for total compliance and lacked the corps du ballet spirit. So I tossed the tutu but kept that fabulous posture and segued to a modern and interpretative dance which was liberating. Run by Miss Solomon who was once an on-the-verge prima ballerina who really was an exceptional modern dancer way before her time. Rumour had it because of that she became a 'black swan' dancer and was never included where and when she needed to be in order to have made dance performance a career. Headstrong, resolute, she went her own way and opened up her unique studio.

Despite being a renegade, Miss Solomon insisted on barre work, center floor work and all manner of the traditional ballet warm-up. But then, forty-five minutes in, the magic began. The lights would dim, the piano accompanist began a quiet, vamp till in the background and Miss Solomon would talk about this or that – about the advent of snow, or falling leaves or how stars look. One by one, she shut the flood lights and lit a spotlight, filmed with different colored gels. She would then nod to her pianist and the musical improvisation part of the hour began. Off we all went into imaginative, creative, untethered dancing in a room soaked in turquoise and sunrise pinks courtesy of the theatrical lights. For me, it was magical and better than just magical, it was total freedom. I could finally get lost only to finally find myself.

Once the music stopped we froze, holding our poses, caught in the act of being a star or fire or a beautiful tree. Once the regular lights came back on, I would scarcely remember where I once. Miss Solomon clapped for all of us and I felt myself sprout wings.

I abandoned studio dance classes at sixteen when dating supplanted ballet. Still I would dance but this time under the midnight moon, after dates, whether they had gone well or not. I danced in Keds and jeans with an inner playlist. No matter how romantic a night I thought I had, dance took me to another, often higher place. Then I got involved in local theatre and this time returned to the dance floor in amateur productions of *Hello Dolly* and *Guys and Dolls*. I danced even when I had my first son, reluctantly leaving him in the YMCA daycare adjacent the dance room for sixty precious minutes while I took jazz classes.

And then the dancing stopped. First it was due to a difficult and lonely marriage that got wonkier with each year and my very, core liveliness faded until it was blunted to nothing. I simply couldn't be the wife I had to be to survive being with *him* and also be who I was. After that, single or solo parent life stopped me in my tracks. The larger truth to both these feeder reasons was that I forgot who I was. While no one ever told me to stop dancing at any point, the forces against were just too great. Or so I thought. The modern jazz class for former dancers didn't do it for me and I saw no other dance possibilities until tango. Tango has brought me back and now, thanks to tango, I have a place to be a dancer again although the biggest challenge here is allowing myself to be led. I've never been led and the business of allowing it or letting go seems close to impossible. Everywhere else in my life I'm directly traffic and reconfiguring the flow.

Like so many dancers, I've always been a solo practitioner but now, as the saying goes, it takes two to tango. It's team work. Tango notwithstanding, I am back to myself. Dance-wise, suddenly I realize there are also *endless* possibilities. There's West Coast Swing, Ballroom and Salsa. Hear this: I will never, ever allow myself to stop dancing ever again.

Hold me closer, tiny dancer
You had a busy day today

Thank you Elton John. I know you're not talking about the tiny dancer in me but your words are still apt. And to quote Jane Bennet in Pride and Prejudice who I think said something along these lines, *I am finally quite back to myself.*

INTERLUDE

PRELUDE TO A KISS OR HOW TO FALL IN LOVE IN THIRTY SECONDS

Tango has an unwritten but implicit **Thirty Second Rule** that's the quintessential litmus test of chemistry and compatibility. It's rarely wrong and it's beautifully simple.

Someone asks you to dance and you say *yes.* Then you observe how he takes your hand or doesn't. Does he usher you to the dance floor or walk somewhat ahead and you follow?

Once on the perimeter of the dance floor, he pauses, stands still and faces you. He opens his arms, which is his invitation to the foyer of the house that is him. He accepts your right hand as your palm slips gently floats against his like a feather landing in a unique cradle of fit. Your left hand reaches for his shoulder if his height is similar to your or only a bit taller; it lands on his bicep if he is somewhat taller. An unbreathed sigh settles you into the moment and then you wait. The music hasn't even begun but both of you facing each other are already intimately connected, touching lightly in body-length. You're both standing still, holding a pose that could pass for a human sculpture but for the duet of breathing underneath the surface that reveals two strangers in abeyance. This takes a poise and presence that seems inborn but it's a practiced thing that one hones over time. You neither look away nor look right into the eyes of the man facing you but you're calm and primed despite any tell-tale flutter.

The first few bars of music fill the air. You notice if he immediately starts to dance, leading with that very first note or if he stays motionless, simply listening to the music until it seeps into him and he becomes attuned in himself. You join in as he decides the moment, the exact bar or beat; until he chooses the scuffed space on the dance floor, the aperture between the other couples, *before* taking that first step and you along with him. Does he someone that waits, hearing his own song or does he join the collective of other leaders who move in unison like a collective tango fleet on that same first note? Does he do what's more likely or expected or does he express his own voice from in that very first step?

The two of you are a ship. He's the captain and you are precious cargo or first mate but you have no way of knowing, until the first wind fills those sails if he is able to navigate whatsoever.

Now all of him is comes towards you in a sensation of new male person. You're close enough to take in the hair at his collar bone if he has any, his shave or lack thereof, his sideburns and the texture of his skin. You see the base of his throat and his Adam's apple and pulse of his breath and tattoo of his heart which beats in denial to how calm and impassive he seems on the outside. Perhaps you preen quietly knowing it comes partly from the mandate ahead of him and partly from the very nearness of you. It might not be you specifically but whatever it is, at this moment it comes packaged in you and that's something you can hold onto.

You breathe in gently and test the air between you, subtly inhaling or cologne or laundry soap or starch or him. You delicately, covertly test the scent to see if you can live with it for three minutes of the dance of longer than that. You assess the scent and determine if he is someone to dance with or a man you could make love to. Not that you will but it's this primal thing, the if-you-had-to, would you? You hear his breath and feel his heartbeat. You wonder if he hears your own heart race as you try and still it. You are a *tanguera* and you don't show your cards but you hope for the best. Much of this is sheer nerves and not romance but it's always there, unpronounced but obvious.

Some men's hands are cold and clammy especially with a new person or your own might be just as clammy but you never transmit that you're aware not even as a light joke to lighten the mood or break the silence. You feel him accepting the shape of your body, your breasts where they touch his chest in an intimacy that is undeclared as it is tacit. No one says a word; instead there's silence, befuddlement and calm all at once.

Some men may smile politely without meeting your eyes or smile and look away, studiously checking out the line of dance ahead. To do more is to commit and no one will avow more than this before the Thirty-Second Rule is passed. To smile dilutes the tension and the mystique and not-knowingness.

As the dance begins all bets are off and all notions are simply this and thought in a split second: can he lead me, can he take care of us, and can I trust this human being to guide me on the floor, take me on a tango adventure and bring me back? Will he protect me from the other dancers, the hard shoulders of men leading other women, and the dagger points of other women's shoes that can pierce my instep? Does he intuitively know what I prefer or is he aware as it all unfolds of what I can do? Is his style gentle or quick; does he cram each bar of music with steps or is he confident enough to wait for the music and its nuances. Does his mood and sensibility wait for me to let me catch up, respond or attune myself? Does he dance *with* me or for the other men so he can impress or does he dance to be *with* me or with us? Does he gloss over his/our mistakes and casually chuckle or cluck his tongue in exasperation? How *present* is this person? Most vital: are we in a conversation, caught between listening and responding or are we each in our own orbit in a strange collision that is a battle or vague compliance.

All this data is swirling and tabulating ten seconds into the dance and you're barely out of the tango harbor. You adjust your touch on his right hand side and move your hips to contour his, aligning the distance and discrepancies between height and body type. You catch a tiny second wind. Now he's no longer a stranger. You've moved into his country and passed from visiting diplomat to native. He gave you a passport when he asked you to dance.

The music continues in phrases, melody and chorus, all in its own subtext. You begin to relax slightly. You realize there's a concordance of style and skill. You don't have to worry for you're in safe hands, if not yet tango's Promised Land.

If he's nervous but a new dancer, you change roles. Instead of him guiding you, you guide him in leading you. You accept him as is and go somewhat limp, verging on acquiescence but maintaining a vestige of spine so he can find a reciprocal intention and energy. Even if he's a novice you can tell he has tango potential but you still give yourself over to his tutoring as he leads you. One day he might be another sort of contender and that's worthy of patience and respect so you respond to the potential that might be there as well as the pride. The tension eases but the dynamics stay.

Twenty more seconds pass and you understand his move and his style. What was a surprise a few moments ago is now a pace and a habit. He repeats a series of steps and what was experimental in a series of doled commands and responses now takes on a finesse. You react well and feel him relax as he intuits that you understand his tango lexicon. He tries something else and you follow in a swathe. There's never a fumble until he introduces a turn you could not anticipate and you jockey again for position, to regain equilibrium, adjusting *just* that much more. In that moment, maybe you allow him to hold you a bit closer. Now you move with an increasing familiarity to better, more common ground. With newly set intention, the dance continues and an aura of deliberation overlays each move. You no longer know where your perfume and his scent begin; it mingles. You no longer notice the difference in height and the lines of his body are now merged with the borderlines of your own as things blur from the he/she place into a new country of 'we'.

The thirty-second mark nears and there's a fit. You're not only safe but you're accepted. You feel his slight relief and appreciation behind the neutral expression which doesn't matter because *you* know that *he* knows you're a match for him. And *he* knows that *you* know that you passed and both of you are now in tango's inner circle.

Such thirty-second dances birth a set of two, three, more such dances. You unconsciously file him in the back recesses of your *Better Tango Partners or Special Dances* list. You've found someone to fall in love with for three dances and be seduced by or seduce, charm, entangle with or share a moment of friendship, albeit all in dance, because you chose to. Tango is the ultimate safe sex and perfect micro romance. You can, if you care to, imagine, for as many bars of music as you need, he is The One. Or you can imagine the one you truly love and truly desire but is not in your life (they have left or not yet appeared), is instead there, already you'll likely never explore. It's enough you are finally in the dock of the bay of connection. This feeling lasts as long as the music plays and it's all you want and need. You don't even need this to happen all the time – just here and there to prove the magic exists and is at hand when you least expect it. Over time you're likely to forget all these things and just be glad of the connection of tango which is where it starts and ends.

The dances wind down and the *cortina* plays. The *tanda* is done. He nods and with more of a smile this time but his eyes meet yours. His slight bow and thank-you is his way of saying, *Another time – we will dance again. I will remember you.* Like thieves sharing magic, it's all sotto voit and sotto emotion - so sweet it's a caress that makes your heart arch. There's no hurry. You'll dance with him again perhaps and pray/hope/wish the alchemy repeats in another thirty-second romance that teases your spirit and slakes your soul. And if he never returns or does and the magic is gone, then there's always another tango bus on the way.

You generally don't but you still might notice who else he dances with after you and if he holds her quite the same way or shares precisely the same touch or if they have the same rapport. You tell yourself it is different with you and them and keep the experience, quickly becoming a myth, alive for a little longer.

And that is how you fall in love in thirty seconds.

CHAPTER THREE

DESPERATELY SEEKING TANGO

I think I'm getting better at tango or at least, I'm not as bad as I was. That being the case, a few nights ago I finally ventured out to a soirée held in the same ballroom where my courses are given. This seems to be the next level in tango: taking your tango show out on the road without the insurance of the classroom safety net. For my intended first bold forays out I've decided it's prudent to stick to my own tango studio and happily they have two soirées a week, one that is somewhat formal and one that is more so and that's where the ringers also show up although I am just beginning to understand all this.

By day, tango schools are not that inspiring but at night they heat up. Darker lighting takes over and little tea-lights are put out on the café tables and the bar opens up. The class wallflowers and the Walter Mitty men transform into divas and Prince Charmings and everything has an altered cachet. Unlike the class environment, where you have a regular or default partner (although you rotate during the class) at a soirée a woman sits and waits. Certainly a woman may ask a man to dance but given the ratio of men (far less) to women (far more) it's generally more strategic (in my playbook at least) to be asked. I'm also relatively new and I'm still quaking in my boots lest someone who's far more experienced asks me to dance and I can't follow or fumble or simply, in my own estimation, fail. So I sit and observe and take it all in.

I've learned to imitate the more experienced tango women and try to look gracious yet purposeful as I sit as if I'm *not* waiting to be asked to dance whatsoever! I'm hope I look impassive on the outside and if I do it's because I've spent time polishing that veneer. It's unlikely that anyone knows that I'm usually doing a mental count of how many men and how many women are in the ballroom and as if I don't subtly resent each extra woman that glides into the ballroom, she herself pretending not to scout the terrain.

It's also probably not apparent because if in life, everyone is self-absorbed, then in tango it's all the more so. The sisterhood is for the office, in the parks with the strollers or in the supermarket. At tango, it's each woman for herself and all the ammunition black fishnet and three inch spikes will allow. I find myself unobtrusively studying each woman's style on the dance floor. I'd like to say I'm bigger than all this but the truth is I'm not there yet. I'm admiring and envious if another woman dancer is particularly adept; I feel rivalrous if she's at the same level. I feel a bit superior if she dresses well but doesn't move with that catlike, sinewy elegance that's so prized. She may have the dress but not the 'look' and yet who's dancing? She is! I've quickly learned that in the end, it's not always about looks or age or fancy shoes or even what the ballroom world calls *floor craft*. You'd think it would be about dance skill or dance chemistry but from what I can tell, there's no rhyme or reason to it. Someone dances more and someone dances less and the whole thing can change the next night out or at a different venue with the same usual suspects. It's a complete mystery to me as much as the full moon and how it evolves on any single night is a strange alchemy you can never forecast or outwit.

Fortunately I usually have partners to dance with although there are some quieter nights. On those occasions I can only embrace the fact that the least I'm acquiring new poise. To sit still with neither a book nor scroll your cell phone and just wait as if it's the most delightful pastime in the world is a foreign state of being. The wellness blog I read calls it 'presence'; I call it crazy-making but these days I can master it to some extent. I reassure myself that I can last an hour like this, just enjoying the music. And if it doesn't pan out as I would like then I'll reward myself with some fancy, heavily whipped cream-topped coffee at a drive-thru on the way home. Win, win.

In the beginning, and this is true of most new *tangueros*, one is fearful that if you are a woman follower you will not follow well; if you're a male leader, you hope you'll be confident and clear. Here, in French, the woman is called, la guidée (the follower or the person being guided), the man, *le guideur* (the leader or guider). A leader gently guides, not forces a follower to match his flow of movement. A follower may look submissive but in actual fact, she's purposeful, elegant and allows herself to be led as a thoroughbred horse, responding best to a gentle and practiced lead, taking her time, doing small embellishments of steps, turns and pauses. I think it's all about the pauses frankly.

I'm totally aware how sexist it all sounds but then, tango is nothing if not sexist in a myriad of ways that are also always evolving especially as the community is so diverse. But for myself I've decided if I don't accept that notion of inherent sexism tango (and social dance in general) and I (a heterosexual woman) will be waging a war for a long time.

Santiago, one of my first teachers often says a woman, no matter what dynamics of sexism are at play always has wherewithal and the power. One night he demonstrated how a woman can get a down-in-the-dumps partner to stand upright and lead her better and essentially rising to the occasion. Santiago would say, in his Latin-accented French, *"Never say: look, Juan is dancing with 'her". Instead say, Pepita is dancing with.....'him", that mec, that guy. Pepita is the star, not him!"*

Treat a woman poorly on the dance floor and what does that make you?" he continued and paused with a knowing, dramatic glance, *"Treat her like a queen and what are you? A king. A king!"* Words to dance by; words to live by although of course Santiago is old school and I'm not sure everyone has his same script but it appeals to me somehow. I'm a divorced woman, mother of three sons: I can stand a little courtship even in three-minute increments.

Unconsciously and somewhat offensively I suppose I'm beginning to think of the various men, *les guideurs*, as the horse handlers. I now know in a few seconds, the difference between gentle touches, hurried touches, nervous, hyper, unconfident, confident, smooth and clumsy touches. Different horse handlers and a different response from me as I became acclimatized to a new handler.

I'm also beginning to see how obsessive tango can be. Maybe many of us start by taking tango to look for romance but you can see us newbies evolve to different stages in our tango-hood and I am pushing through those stages rapidly as the months go on.

Stage One is what I call the *Tango Virgin.* Starry eyed, hopeful - each man that asks you to dance is a potential romance. You are almost loath to dance with someone else if the dance chemistry is there. And then you learn it's only a dance. The music stops and the magic stops too until the music begins again and someone else comes round. You invest in another three-minute romance and then move on. You nod *merci*, deliver the most siren of smiles that never reaches your eyes, and evaporate off the dance floor. If it's surprisingly a good dance with a new person, you wait as the dance ends. *Un autre,* an other? *Mais oui, but yes,* and you try another go-round. The best dancers need at least three, four dances to get used to each other and experienced tango dancers know this which is also the theory (I think) behind the *tanda*, the set of three or four dances you do with each partner.

You never say 'I'm sorry' when you step on a man's toes but a man that bumps his partner into another couple? He's immediately apologetic and contrite. *So sorry, my fault,* he will say. *No matter*, you demure. Sometimes you don't even register that you noticed the fumble. Everything is cool and even the imperfections are recorded as choreographed perfection.

Stage Two is the *Tango Tigress.* More confident, the *Tango Tigress* asks any man in the room to dance. She stalks the best-looking, best dancing male and just asks. She barely registers the rare "*non*".

And then there's the *Numbers Game Tango* which refers to those of us who will dance with anyone just to say the evening went well and their dance card was full. We're all like that at times and more so in the beginning. But then one starts getting fussy.

This is when you segue to the *Tango Empress,* the queen, the diva of dance. Tango builds your self-esteem and you decide who you want to dance with, if you want to dance or simply listen to the music, even, and this is real evolvement, chat at the bar with another, bright woman than dance with a guy you're not drawn to.

I recently met Nicole that way, a real estate agent and municipal counselor. We got to talking one night at a tango festival sometime in Montreal's summery extravaganza of festivals, tango and otherwise.

"*You know,* said Nicole, pointing out several men we both had danced with over the weeks, "*Tango is the dance of non-commitment. All these guys have commitment problems. Salsa? Tried that. That's the dance of the thirty-something and promiscuous. Very Latin.*" Nicole said sagely. "*And swing? For twenty-somethings, no complexes, mainstream people*".

I'm not sure I agree with Nicole's views and so far I can't declare that tango is for men who can't commit. But I have to concede it does entice the most intellectual and/or bohemian of men. Artists, doctors, musicians, writers, programmers, veterinarians. It takes an independent man to come to tango. Women seem to come more easily and come from more traditional professions because dance to most women is like ducks to water. It's in our DNA. People expect women to show up in dance classes whereas men are seen to be braver to come on their own.

In my second soirée of tango, I met André, who I thought was a French Canadian painter. He was a painter, but he turned out to be of Moroccan Jewish descent. He was pleasant albeit compulsive about getting each step right and often full of apologies and self-reproach. One night, I said gently, *André, take it easy, it is only a dance. We are here to have fun.*

He replied, *"A few years ago, my wife and three daughters died in a car accident on the highway. I dance to forget. In one instant, I lost my whole world. Tango, even for one hour, is the only relief from that pain I get".*

After that I said little but let him self-efface and micro-manage to his heart's content.

Another man I danced with, dark haired, around late thirties with earnest, almond-shaped eyes always seem to have a creak in his shoulder which was quite audible as he led me. I teased him and asked, 'what ***is*** that sound? A sports injury or old age?" He told me: *I spent two years in an Iraqi prison for social dissidence when I was studying to be a doctor. They beat me often and my friends every day. I was the only one that made it out.*

In my third session of tango I noticed there were fewer couples that already knew each other. Gone were the engaged couples learning a dance step for their wedding reception, the couples trying to recapture a togetherness activity or the singles seeking romance who disappeared after *Tango One. Tango Three* was strictly tango and it's filled with a fleet of dedicated tangueros who were there to get better at the dance they loved. Everyone enters the studio with a warm salute of *hola* and a continental kiss on each cheek. My partner in this session was Henrick, a young saxophonist who introduced me to a more refined style no doubt part of his training as a jazz musician. He was all about subtlety and timing. Sometimes I danced with a middle-aged psychiatrist who seems to be at a similar stage of tango-hood as me but chatted incessantly throughout each dance, ruining all sense of rapport, flattening the connection with his chatter, ensuring no magic could ever occur.

Like bowls of porridge, you try different partners. This one moves too quickly, this one dances too close, this one is too repetitive and this one is just right.

What about tango clothes? That seems to be simple enough. Tango clothes are inevitably black for men and women. If you want more colorful I guess you'd go to salsa class but at tango it's black and more black. It's either classic black or vintage style and overall, it's minimalist, somewhat fancier at night than for classes but variations on a theme. Here no one seems to be flamboyant. This is not a frothy ballroom venue and I observe how the subtle, well-fitted styling only serves to showcase the dancing that much more than coordinated movement to music. Some places are more Avant guard and the styles are more street, Boho and non-binary but so much of the time it's fifty shades of...... black.

As you'd expect perfect, incomparable, seductive, beautifully crafted tango shoes are in demand. Women covet each other's shoes. Not that there's really time and occasion to ask, but no one really shares where they get their shoes. Some murmur of bringing footwear from Argentina or having bought a pair or two when last in Buenos Aires on a tango junket. There are high-heeled shoes and lower-heeled ones as well as some pairs of Nikes or Tom are snuck in for practice times but usually your footwear pronounces your fashion style and tango skills at the same time. There are of course Capezio character shoes but mostly in beginner classes or practicas.

Most nights I can rely on tango as the tonic for my daily life of car pools and testing recipes but sometimes it can be a bit much what with the divorce lawyer and initial separation difficulties. At those times, it's difficult even for tango to coax me out of my mood. Sometimes, I can be simply too tired. The tango ballroom can become just a din of shuffling feet on the dance floor and snatches of conversations drifting over the clink of glasses, all set against a never-ending minor key of a tango classic that is inevitably about love's disappointment or betrayal or dangerous and sad passion.

On those occasions, I begin to wonder what I am doing, trying to build this *just-for-me* oasis with people who all seem, in contrast to me, footloose and fancy free. And *just* as I am descending into the '*what am I doing here*' spiraling line of thinking, suddenly someone I thought was making their way to the bar stops at my table. A hand is outstretched and there's no point looking behind me – it's clearly for me. A man gently inquires in a voice that is quiet but discernable above the music, *"Madame, voulez-vous dancer?"* He tilts his head in an inquisitive nod. Without hesitation, I let myself be escorted like a swan to a special pond to a reserved spot on the dance floor. He opens his embrace and allows me to settle into place. I feel myself adjust to a new physique and the subtle scent of a stranger who will be my next, new time-centric minute romance. We stand in that starchy pre-dance tableau and then the music starts and the dance begins.

Suddenly I'm in flight and that thing called joy inflates wings I didn't know were still there – understudies of my happy spirit that was just in hiding. I'm no longer on the periphery of the ballroom or the periphery of life but in the inner circle of both. This seems to happen again and again- that wellspring of magic that just keeps regenerating and bringing me back.

What can I tell you? I'm all in.

At the next milonga/soiree I'm decanting the higher heels. If I fall, someone will catch me. That much I know is a sure thing.

CHAPTER FOUR

RUSHING TO TANGO

Tick tock, tick tock: without fail, my inner tango alarm goes off every three days and when it does I experience near-narcotic tango withdrawal symptoms. Fortunately these symptoms coincide with the next scheduled practica or a class so relief is on the way. Said withdrawal is evidenced by a twitch of the neck and limbs, a craving for sweets, a shorter-than-usual temper and a pervasive resistance to the reality of the present moment which is to say: *all* the moments I'm not at tango. Tango might be legal cocaine, a fat-free candy and a ticket-less speeding ticket but it's a compulsion nonetheless. It makes everything between it and *not* it a steeple-chase wherein you only see the end game which is to be back in tango class.

And so it starts:

It's time - time to get ready.
Tripping over homework and notes from school.
Forgot to make something for supper. Forgot to get money to leave for pizza.
Getting money for pizza. Overseeing argument of which pizza place.

On top of that I forgot to hand in the feature on herbal teas and gluten-free biscotti to *Food and Wine,* the pitch on low-fat Greek Yogurt cheesecake for *Bon Appetit.* It all has to wait. Also on the wait list are the edits on the cookbook with the new editor that really hates me because she was forced to inherit me when she took over the new imprint. Damn and damn again. I showered and yet my hair still smells of vanilla, tell-tale signs of my day job testing butter cookies because on this end it's always Christmas in July. Now I'm truly sweating underneath my fresh clothes being legitimately *just* out of the shower which does nothing to help me dry my naturally frizzy, curly hair. Just one night a week, I want it to look …nice or at least normal.

I'm late. I'm late. I'm late

Time to shower ; hair takes ages and now due to sweaty-stress it will take longer to dry and while it sounds silly, no one at tango has yet seen me with curly hair. I'm still pretending to be perfect.

I hear noise and turn the drier off; it's ok. It's only the boys fighting or the boys fighting again. Don't ask, don't tell, and don't (yet) have to intervene. HOW DO THEY KNOW I AM LATE AND HAVE TO, HAVE TO, HAVE TO go to tango? How do they always time it so perfectly?

Crave it. Miss it. Waited 6 days, 11 hours, and 22 minutes to get ready to do it all again. Tapping my toe all week just to get to this point again where time is compressed onto a pinhead which is more real than the entire rest of my reality.

Feet twitch and flex – I cannot dry hair fast enough! I already have the slinky black skirt on (perfect swish-to-slink ratio). My day-wear uniform of a Gap tee-shirt floats up and off and a swath of black stretch dotted Swiss lace does the honors and last rites. Makeup is minimal. No time. Screw up the eye makeup. Have to start over. Hear more sounds of boys' voices squalling over the dryer noise.

STOP FIGHTING!!!
There's more pizza. No hockey in the living room.
Do you hear me?
And then A Note on the Stairs From School.
The Grade 3 Bake Sale tomorrow *- which means:*
I'll be baking at 5 am or at midnight. Whichever is less impossible.
"Why didn't someone tell me about the bake sale?"

THIS ALWAYS HAPPENS.
I'm the only professional baker the school has ever seen and I'm chronically late for the bake sale. Go figure. Late for notes signed. Late to return library books, late to leave out water bottles for the water guy delivery and late to put out the recycling bin. Late for this, late for that. Now late for tango.

By the way no one else in tango seems to have children. If they do, they have one child. This child is inevitably a Thirty-Year Old Documentary Film Maker Now Living in Spain that they see every other summer having divorced their spouse 16 years ago when the boy was a teenager. I know what you're thinking: how is it *possible* that everyone at tango collectively, has the same film-making son, living far off in Madrid where the light, apparently is so much better for documentary films. I don't know but they do. One thing is for sure: no one has more than one child and no one but me lives with three boys that only see tango as the rival for their affections and needs. No one does car pool, nor bake sales nor shops for juice boxes on sale.

Why does she go to tango? What happened to her? Where is 'old mom"?

Ok - almost done and almost on my way

Kisses – some land on a cheek, at least two get blown into the air.
How do I look?
Fine.
No one looks.
Sounds of Dorito bags being crunched.
Cell phone on but on vibrate.

Bye, good bye, bye.
No answer.
BYE!

GOOD-BYE! Three voices, in unison, and all equally loud, shout it back.
GO ALREADY. You are driving us nuts.

But no gas in car. Ugh! Get gas
Get on the road - hit a wall of traffic. It is not even rush hour what is this traffic

Detour now. A detour!! I am late, late, late!

I will have my partner waiting there and Laurent the best tango teacher in the world will say,

Eh bien, Andre, and where is Marcy?"

Andre will have to sit out. Jocelyne will dance with him, taking turns from her partner, toggling back and forth between two worthy swains.

Andre will no doubt fall in love with Jocelyne whilst I'm gone and decide she is a far better partner than me anyway. I can just see it now.

Next week, he'll probably refuse to dance with me. He'll glide around with Jocelyne and I will have to sit out or they will have to call an 'extra' (the guys who fill in) to come in.

Oh, that cat, Jocelyne. I may have once liked her but now I hate her! In my mind, in my dreams, in this blasted, stupid traffic on the detour I decide that Jocelyne is an awful woman that is just waiting in the wings to steal Andre from me since the fall session. I knew it!

Breathe in, breathe out. Find some Celtic waterfall music. Inhale two Tic Tacs.

Traffic is flowing. Finally. How cruel was that? I remember car clock is 6 minutes ahead. I can make it. I know I can make it. Almost a smile; I feel my breath begin to regulate.
Factor in three minutes to put on dance shoes. The equation works. I can make it.

Arrive. Find parking spot. Perfect. But: no money for parking meter. I could scream.
I want to screech. All I WANT TO DO IS GO TO TANGO CLASS!
WHY IS THIS SO DAMNED HARD?

It's a sign. That's it. A sign that single mothers of three sons have no business leaving the suburbs on a Wednesday night to go to tango class. I should have gone to the Yankee Candle party, the Tupperware night or the Japanese Four Season Tea Ceremony thing at the museum I promised I would take my mother to.

See what you get for wanting a life?

I dig out four quarters and I feed the meter's mouth and it belches up parking time in return. Race to tango with mincing heels clicking away on the pavement. Two construction workers just stare. I AM A DANCER, can't you see that? Get over it. I tap my way down the street and follow the yellow brick road. Now what? It's raining! Drat drat drat – all that hair blow-drying for nothing.

Two valet parking attendants, standing outside a steak restaurant eye me with idle interest, one debates whistling but catching the hell-bent-for-leather glint in my eye thinks otherwise.

Only, "*Bonjour Madame. Bon soirée*

Oui. Merci. Bonne soirée, monsieur, vous même.

Up the stairs, my heart clamoring like a horse who knows she is getting to go out for a longer gallop without a saddle and the prospect of dry, crisp, verdant fields with limitless trails. I go up the second flight of stairs and through the hallways, around the corner, to the voice like a metronome. Is that from *A Chorus Line* or my own thoughts?

The doors are open and I see people moving but not yet dancing! I don't hear anything specific (like a teacher's voice) but there's some low talking. The music hasn't started yet. Turns out: I am on time! I haven't missed anything! No one even realizes that I'm frantic with the thought I'm late. I notice Joseph (kind, inevitable Joseph, the class veteran) stroll in after me. Joseph, coming in *after* me legitimizes me and frames me as being 'just on time' and I finally begin to calm down.

I smile at Jocelyne. She's wearing the pink and black print skirt she wore the first class. *You know, I really like her. I am sorry I thought those things about her. Where does she get those mesh stockings anyway? I must ask her.*

Ah, Andre, partner of mine. Like an old pair of slippers, we know each other so well.
Voulez-vous dancer? Yes, Mais oui.
And yes, again yes.
Pouvez-vous me chauffer avant notre class commence?

I am dancing! How I have missed this! I made it to tango class on time! There *is* a god and his name is Astor Pizzaolla and he hates both Celtic Waterfall music and Gotan Project.

I breathe and sink it Andre's arms. You see, you can do that at tango. No one minds. In fact, it's how it's done. It is the ultimate catch-me-when-I-fall-human net. You just lean back and let someone else drive. You just mind your own lane.

Andre says, *"How was your week?" Comment c'était?*

I melt and I smile. We turn and nimbly elude hitting Jocelyne and her partner, Renaldo.
I like Renaldo well enough and I'll inherit him at the next partner switch. He's taller than Andre but I like Andre better and familiarity breeds content.

"My week was fine. Et vous?" becoming the French (and infinitely nicer) version of myself.

Class begins. All is calm. All is bright. All is right. I love tango; I love this world and I love life. I'll eat cold pizza later tonight while I bake Tollhouse cookies-without-nuts-because-of-kids-with-allergies (mine!) for the bake sale at five am.

I don't care. I'm finally dancing. Someone pinch me. This is so wonderful. It is, and I loathe using this word for anything but food: but it's utterly delicious.

Oh god.
It's my cell phone.
Shit. I can hear the tell-tale vibrations across the room where it sits in my EBay Birkin replica handbag. The boys are fighting and

their May Day call is breaking through into this lovely world reminding me of that in another lovely-but-in-a-different-way world that is my default world that all is *not* ok.

On the end of that cell phone is pure chaos and I can't control it remotely.

Shit
Shit
Shit

I turn off phone. Demurely nod to class. Return to my place in the tango circle as we stand around, listening to dance notes.

Breathe. Inhale. Dance. Live. I wonder if maybe one day, all three boys might consider becoming film makers in Spain where apparently the light is better.

And it's:
One, two, three, four…and we are off!

Bon voyage, tangueros, says the teacher.

I smile into the right shoulder of my partner, smile, and take my place and ticket on that one-way tango voyage that takes me far away and yet seems to bring me home again and again while touching down on with lighter feet. I am dancing and all is well.

Hola, Houston, we have no problems. Tango One is launched and on its way.

INTERLUDE

THE SUBJECT WAS SHOES

There's only one thing rarer than a perfect tango partner and that is a pair of perfect tango shoes. Shoes, pardon the pun, are pivotal.

Both my closet and trunk of my car are home to many pairs of worn-out shoes that sport evidence of the many tango miles I've traveled. This also includes a few pairs not even worn in. The more-used shoes have dusty soles that are unevenly broken in, indications of where I habitually lean this way or that. They brag dusty streaks on the leather where I might have had an argument with the *piste de dance* or lost my balance while landing a turn. There are nicks on the black suede of other pairs where another *tanguera's* steps might have scuffled with mine or I've been led astray by a partner who was sloppy with his lead. As a consequence I brushed too close to a table leg or a support column. In the case of the latter, the support column predictably didn't yield to my stretched leg as I kicked backwards in a dramatic gaucho. I hid the limp until after the dance was done. I walked casually off the floor and then scurried from the ballroom to the coat room to repair and wait for the throbbing to stop.

There are shoes once new and pulsing with potential that now have a dull patina of milongas past. In the worn buckle holes the crafted leather seams there are untold tales of long nights of tango that went well or badly or toggled between both extremes. If I listen closely, I can almost hear the echo of laughter like silver chimes, as well as smell the smoke of unfiltered cigarettes from the hallway and taste the dry, Chilean wine or a domestic beer. In this same aura of memory I can feel that gentle breeze, a thoughtful courtesy of the wind that floated in on any given summer night. The breeze might also come from the phantom flutter of the women's Chinese paper fans as they sat, waiting to be asked to dance.

The tango shoes speak and smell of wood dance hall floor, male sweat, women's perfume and a little hunger. Lying quietly on the closet floor, neatly lined up beside the shoes of everyday life, the tango shoes purr proudly and dominate the shoe venue that is the bottom of my wardrobe. Everything is potent with its unique vibration.

These shoes have stories to tell and midnight secrets. My other work-a-day, regular life shoes are quiet in response. What could they possibly say?

I sometimes wonder if the different shoes eye each other in the same furtive competitiveness some of the tango women eye their sisters. Each shoe has its place but the tango shoes seem rogue among the Nikes, cowboy boots and summer sandals. *We serve too*, they say. *Agreed,* rejoin the tango shoes, *but who gets to go to the dance? "We've covered dollar store shops, the mall and circled Ikea linens countless times!"* protest the daytime-life shoes but the tango shoes don't seem to listen or care.

It almost goes without saying for it seems so obvious, but the true soul of tango is strung on a base note which is found, as you would expect on the soles of your feet. Without the right shoes you simply can't focus on the dance. If you're worried about basics like your own two feet, your ankles and terra firma then you cannot possibly begin to trip the light fantastic in the hallowed halls of dance. Instability, new-shoe blisters as well as slipping on the floor do little to create or empower your tango or make you a legend even to yourself. You need/you want/you have to be able to focus on the *dance* and the connection. If you're at all pre-occupied about the mechanics then you can't get lost in the embrace or otherwise disappear into the place you so crave.

In a way, shoes are *everything* (style, price, fit, look, uniqueness) *until* that moment you put them on. Then they are forgotten save for an occasion that some other woman admires them. The dancing is all that matters.

Shoes signal so many things, real, false and imagined but possibly true.

Lower shoes signify safety, a newbie, tired feet, a prioritizing of comfort over looks. Higher, prettier shoes signify sexiness, a prowess, experience or it could be as simple as needing to make up a height differential. Some things true, some are not and some are reasonable conjecture. Low shoes take a certain confidence (you know yourself and want to be comfortable) and higher ones take the same (you know yourself and are comfortable being glamourous with a higher view and statement shoes).

There are some basics but even these things change over the years as trends come and go. It used to be the higher the shoe, the better, or at least, more experienced the dancer. Beyond that, the women wearing them were considered skilled and perhaps even sensuous on and off the dance floor. Packaging does go a long way in making a first impression but then you do have to carry it off beyond that first impression.

This isn't to say that experienced dancers also don't take the lower heel sabbatical once in a while or tango teachers don't teach in jazz sneakers but few newbies risk the high wire of tango on stilts at the outset. In tango, if you splurge at first for the towering shoes based on looks versus your particular ability to manage them you might hurt yourself quite badly but it's all an experience and we each learn it in our own ways. Everyone comes with extra shoes although it's rare anyone changes their shoes mid-evening.

The more patent, more red, more suede, and overall more exotic the shoe – the more sensual, confident and unique the dancer. It's also more likely she has also been to Buenos Aires where she bought the shoes and furthered her tango or has somehow discovered all the secret places in the city or online to find 'just-so-perfect' shoes. Of course, it can work the other way as well. Shoes, no more or less than one's clothes, shouldn't upstage the person themselves. It's *really* about your dance and personality that should do the talking. That said, superb shoes are a calling card although it depends on who's looking on the outside in.

In my closet, at any point in time, it seems like I have plenty of tango shoes but yet not one pair seems to do at times! I've shopped EBay, countless tango shoe website, ordered custom shoes from a family in Argentina and a custom shoe place in Connecticut where the tango shoes are designed by a former dancer. In the end, I barely have 1-2 pairs that keep me in flight. Why is this? It is at once personal and generic.

For starters, what are perfect tango shoes? For my money they should be somewhere between a lady and a vixen: built for comfort, designed to swirl, stomp, stamp, swoon, and seduce. But one's first tango shoes are generally a serviceable pair of dance character shoes or Mary Janes of some sort. They might not be officially 'tango' shoes but they should have a strap on them.

You might not feel that graceful in them at first but you also don't feel you are going to tip over or be forced to lean too much on your partner. It takes about two sessions of tango or about one year to invest in new shoes that are a bit more interesting and that purchase marks your inauguration from a tango newbie (generic) into the fledging (but unique) tango version of you.

Heel height: this is very important. Adjusting shoe heels/height to men of your class, practica and/or your regular partner, nay, anticipating the majority height for any given tango evening or event, this takes planning. It also takes back up heels you leave in the car or tango cloakroom.

If I'm at a place where I might not know anyone and therefore care less about impressions, I'm more likely to test out new shoes. Silly but true; there's less to risk when you're in a strange new land.

Shoe inserts are helpful and even though the name Dr. Scholl doesn't jam in a nice way with the word tango, you are wise to find foam or gel inserts for your shoes. If you dance *with* stockings, you will need the inserts that much more. Personally, I can't fathom how people dance with pantyhose because your feet slide so badly that way. Speaking of feet, *don't* have a pedicure on the *day* of tango because the polish gets creased and weird but do keep your toes pretty. There will be a moment when you change to street shoes or boots and your feet will be naked. I'm not saying you'll be judged but it's not unwise to celebrate your feet with a wellness routine. Beauty is as beauty does, inside and out.

Shoes have their own partnership issues and the primarily partnership is the dance floor itself. Some floors are sticky, or shiny, tacky, new, sanded, slippery or what not. For slippery you can rosin your shoes (which is frowned on and unless you are tango-ing with a violinist or know about rosin from ballet classes, who has rosin in their purse?). For sticky floors, some tango studios will permit you to toe in a bit of powder or talc but overall this is also frowned on.

In summary, I suggest two to three pairs of shoes: practica shoes which are no-nonsense, scuffed but tried and true, not too high, nor low, and built for comfort. Then you need a classic black pair of medium high heels (Copa, Latin, or Havana heels). Then, on a night when you are feeling confident, mysterious and ready to either fall in love, seduce, haunt a stranger or just impress, you need the highest, meanest shoes possible often called Nuevo tango shoes. Suede, patent trim, some red or electric blue or tone on tone but something that announces you're a contender so dance your heart out. There are times to strut and when it's one of those times, find the shoes that will do the trick.

CHAPTER FIVE

BLIND MAN, DANCING TANGO

There are no mistakes in the tango, not like life.
It's simple. That's what makes the tango so great.
If you make a mistake, get all tangled up, just tango on.

From film Scent of a Woman, starring Al Pacino, screenplay by Bo Goldman

I used see this blind tango dancer every once in a while but I didn't quite notice him in a conscious way. I should have but over time spent on the tango dance floor, you get to know the usual suspects and filter out the rest you're not in much contact with. That's strange because he was the *only* blind tango dancer and that's noticeable but even the fact that he was blind didn't quite make him stick out any more than anyone else. Tango people, even the marginal people (which is to some extent, is everyone at tango), fade into the perimeter wood of the dance floor or become tango wallpaper, a visual surround you only really notice if someone points someone else out for some reason or another and then afterwards, that part of human wallpaper transmutes from an isolated patch into a *person.* The best you can do is usually respond, saying, "*Ah yes, him….the guy* with the one red earring or all the tattoos, or *her,* the one with the red and black patent shoes that *are too tall for her or him, the blind guy*". Now if you have danced with someone you soon begin to know their very touch like every distinct scent your brain has catalogued. That touch, their embrace, becomes a bookmark of a sort. Ever after that you can't look at anyone at tango without simultaneously remembering their tactility along with how they led you. It's a Rolodex of sensations that configure into an overall impression and at that point they've graduated from being wallpaper or part of the dance floor to a *someone.*

It turned out the blind guy/dancer was called Michael. He blended in so well that I first I scarcely noticed he was blind until one day I saw him arrive at tango class by Uber or a cab with a black Labrador service dog in tow. A tango dancer with a black Lab is an image one remembers and of course by implication that pronounces a physical challenge. Arriving by cab is another one because most tango people all seem to walk or bike to tango. Those who live further away take the metro. I'm on the short list of people that drive.

Other longer-time tango students, noticing me notice Michael, would whisper, as he carefully made his way into the room: *Michael, you know, is totally blind but he's been coming to tango for many years. He usually hires a cab but sometimes, Claudine or Carlos brings him or takes him home at times. His dog is adorable and so patient'*

I admit to being more than a bit curious about Michael, having grown up and shared my room when I was a child with my grandmother who was blind. As a sighted person, without being aware of it, you get attuned being around blind people. While it's true, depending on how profound the impairment, that many or most people who are blind can't see *you* by contrast, the *seeing* person, for virtue of having been so much a part of their eyeless sphere, move in their own altered state ever after. That's how it is for those of us who have walked alongside blind people; we take on another skin of awareness ourselves.

One evening, Michael turned up in my *Tango Four* class. Everyone greeted him with hugs and two-cheeked kisses as he seemed acquainted with all of them. His dog, Luna lay obediently at one of the café tables his master installed him at. The dog gave a big sigh, as he anticipated two hours of (at least to a dog, boring) tango music. It was dance time and this service dog settled into his break as his master took to the dance floor. At the partner rotation, I was eventually partnered with Michael. He introduced himself and I discovered his first language was English, rather than French, which made things, at least for me, easier. The music started and we were off.

Michael moved in a studied, deliberate way. He held me closer than the other men, and his cues, as far as the movement of other dancers went was different. He never, ever, once collided with another couple nor bumped me into a wall or furniture.

Other dancers do collide with static objects. It's something that happens and it's not a big deal but Michael had a sixth sense about that. Over time, I began to trust him more, knowing I was safe and together, as a team, we were ok. Sometimes, I caught him smile as we executed one step or another without a mishap. We tried more steps and combinations and had more success. *Are you a dancer*? he asked. *I mean, do you dance aside from tango*? *I can feel it in how you carry yourself.* I was pleased he noticed and said, *yes, I am a dancer.* (Of course, if I had a dime for every guy that says that at dance......)

The instructor stopped the class to offer more counsel. Michael rested his hand on one of my shoulders. I soon learned he preferred to always keep physical contact with his partners, whether they were dancing at the moment or not. It was easy to get accustomed to this as I grew up with a blind person and was intuitively used to it. There's Braille of the skin and the Braille of one's touch.

I also became familiar with Michael's unique way of leading and I also made sure, even when there was a pause in the class, to never move too far away from him. One day I was standing near him but not too close as I was not currently dancing with him as his partner. But he turned and said *Marcy, is that you? Yes, I said* and kissed him hello on both cheeks, oddly, mildly embarrassed I hadn't made my presence known and greeted him earlier on. *How did you guess?* I asked him.

Oh, that is easy. Your perfume. No guessing involved. You always smell like lilacs or lily of the valley or something with jasmine and roses. It is easy to know you. He smiled and said, *even when you're a few feet away I know you're there.*

Ah, I thought, this is territory I know: a man flirting. I smiled. He must have felt or sensed my smile for he gave me a gentle elbow jab. Sometimes I stumbled and Michael would subtly guide me and it was an inverse: blind-man-leading-sighted-woman.

When I mention Michael to other people, they say, *ah ha, just like that scene in Scent of a Woman.* Not really and I want to add *no – that's a movie; that is Hollywood tango.* But I let it pass; Michael wasn't any sort of trope.

I saw Michael some other times after that session and occasionally at other tango schools. I dance with a lot of men and have many other partners as we all do. When a partner of mine has a hard time or the dance floor is particularly traffic-filled, and we bump and collide with other couples, I fob it off because it happens. But I also remember that Michael was blind and he still guided me perfectly. He trusted that the other dancers would not crash into him and he trusted his own dancing. He led me without faltering, navigating from his own inner, uniquely lit world into a dark one. I guess he had learned by then to trust all would be well. It was and we were. Perhaps too, the other dancers were more courteous and gave him wider berth.

At the end of the evening, other tango dancers would bring Michael a glass of water and a bowl of water for his dog. Hugs goodbye and a pat for Lunda and an embrace for Michael. Accompanied by another tango student, they would leave; the other person might drive him home or flag down a cab or his Uber. I liked seeing the other tango dancers transform from followers and leaders into caring friends. It showed me another broader dimension of their humanity.

I always remember how I liked dancing with Michael! He reminded me of that closeness of spirit I shared with my grandmother. I sometimes forget about it but that's a bond you have you don't realize you have until you encounter another blind person and then it all comes back to you.

But the other thing about dancing with a blind man is another lesson entirely. The thing is, and I should know this having lived with a blind person, but more so, for having *danced* with one: some people just have this inner compass that guides them. You worry for them but they are in fact, just fine. In the end, you don't always have to see to lead. You just have to know what you're about one step at a time. You just have to listen and be really present. A sixth sense replaces one of your basic five ones, admirably filling in.

Tango, much like life, is about a hunch about direction. You give it a shot. Then you put one step in front of the other. From a distance, it looks like dancing. From a greater distance, it looks like a straight line. Take it one step further and it almost looks though you know where you are going. If two people do this together, in harmony – well, that is a sight to see. Even a blind man could tell you that.

CHAPTER SIX

THE FOUR SEASONS OF TANGO: AUTUMN GOOD NIGHT TANGO CINDERELLA

The art of knowing when to leave a tango evening is as essential as knowing when to leave a great party. It's a tango credo I pride myself in; it's not only knowing *when* to leave but also *how* to leave as unobtrusively as possible. Like all special things, poised on a moment of serendipitous benevolence, you never want to over-stay your welcome and dissipate the positive experience. Once you expertly master the coming-and-going thing then you get to curate any dance soirée as a tango portrait, framed in perfection, a moment forever catalogued in your memory. I've made it a habit to collect such tango 'artworks' to savor at another time. I used to covet these as one does with the last chocolate in a box of treats, clutching to a sublime memory in fear there'd be a scarcity or no new decadent truffle or ultimate dance to top it. Happily, however, overtime there's been so many dance interludes that have overlapped with each other so now it's become a collage as large as a tango Sistine chapel ceiling. Naturally some moments still stand out more than others.

Some nights this leave-taking is early and some nights, it's definitely Cinderella at the tango ball which is to say it usually occurs when the clock strikes a telling hour and I can barely tear myself away but I have to go. I'm still unmarried-with-sleeping-children at home. Those sorts of nights unroll in beautiful happenstance of one glorious dance after another and everything feels just magical! Your steps are perfect no matter whom you dance with and more often than not, you find yourself dancing with people you never danced with before or total strangers who appeared for the first time ever and you're likely never see again. You manage to harmonize stylistically no matter *who* leads you and there's no mishap or colliding with others. Things just flow.

At these times, I tell myself, *just one more dance, just one more – until they play Le Caprasita.* **Le Caprasita** is a beloved cliché of a tango song that no matter where you dance it's traditionally played as the last song of any tango evening, signifying the final call of the dance floor. When you hear the first chords of *Le Caprasita* you know it's time to quickly grab someone and finish the soirée on a high note. If you glance around you'll witness impulsive and speedy pairings as people find each other and make haste to the dance floor so they don't miss out. Unlike other tango couplings, the priority for the last dance is to dance, not to seek the most skilled or prettiest dancers and people are (happily) less picky. There's that New Year's Eve sensibility about it where you simply don't want to be the only one not dancing or not getting kissed at midnight.

As a rule, tango begins relatively later in the evening all over the globe. Things only get warmed up after ten pm and peak around midnight to one am. On one such night, having listened live to a Nuevo group called *Narco Tango,* I left very late, somewhere around 3:30 am. Even then, judging from the success of the evening (wonderful venue, sublime music mix, many wonderful dancers), was still too-soon. The floor was swarmed with people in the midst of having the best possible time. But I had my own inner cue saying it was both way past the time to leave and also still preserve the magic. I had work the next day and a family to take care of and had stayed long enough as it was. Guilt had set in. I reluctantly and carefully closed the heavy doors of the ballroom as I made my exit, tango shoes and car keys in hand. It had been an incredible night of dance but now it was time to undo tango's sticky tentacles and transform back into my other life.

It was fall and the city was resplendent in falling oak and maple leaves, each one floating down like different-colored jewels that coated the streets. Some were crumpled and wizened and these blew in small whirlpools around my ankles as I stepped outside. The air smelled like fireplaces and cinnamon. It was cold with the type of chill that warns you of winter and only intensifies that feeling of leaving the ball and something ending on a bittersweet note – always too soon, not enough and one moment more and it would be too much which is as much for tango balls as it is for a season ending and a new one awaiting to awake.

Since the event was distant from my suburban nest I was obliged to drive through several districts before I hit the highway that would navigate me back to a place where tango is only a rumor and the strip mall *Arthur Murray* dance franchise rules the roost. Street by street, some narrow and historically old, depending on the district, I toddled my way home, driving quietly in the early morning, like a little she-cat stealing her way so as not to awaken anyone nor stir hidden police in speed traps just waiting to pounce.

Ambling along, I noted the drawn blinds and fabric shades and the dim street, dusky street lamps casting a dull gold on black pavement, outside refurbished industrial buildings now given to hipster start-ups.

I passed second-hand furniture stores, retro bike and camera stores, and an old-fashioned hardware store with a rocking chair in the window and a small dog fast asleep on its seat. Chocolate-colored recycling bins neatly stood at attention, awaiting the 'green' brigade that would pass the next morning. The trees, maple, oak and willow, quietly crooned their nightly lullaby and told the gossip of the street. A foil cigarette paper blew by, fused to some dry leaves from no particular season. There was no one about and I was almost surprised I didn't see tumbleweed float by in a ghostly echo of the blank slate of the streets. Not a sound, not a person, not even a trundling late night city bus interrupted my journey. It could have been a stage set – a mock-up of a city, a backdrop and nothing more, nothing real.

As I drove through the quiet I realized that at some point in time, we all sleep. Even this city that brags about its nightlife and joie de vivre, at some point even the coolest of the cool, they must also rest. Conversely, and for a change, this suburban mother of three was the only one up and that made me smile. I enjoyed the novelty of being the last woman standing in this nocturnal world, freshly transported from one of the most romantic dances in the world.

Finally I made it to the highway and traveled the last miles home more swiftly, more expediently, leaving the City of Nod behind me. Another mile or two and I rounded into my own driveway where I faced my own snoozy house and life. A quiet rumble of the garage door lifted the moat door, I moored my car and I was home.

Key in the lock, put on the alarm, I brewed a quick cup of Earl Grey tea which was left, untouched, fragrant and cooling as I fell into the covers. My tango shoes were strewn on the floor. Like me, they were tired but replete having earned the deep and sweet sleep of shoes that had done their job well. I might have heard them sigh, no doubt the content of a warm fatigue as they settled in. Forgetting the tea, I melted into an instant and profound slumber. I dreamt of sugar plums and car pools, men dressed as black swans and hockey gear strewn in the hallway.

Welcome home Tango Cinderella. Sleep well, tomorrow is another day.

Goodnight to tango and to all, a goodnight.

CHAPTER SEVEN

HOW NOT TO TAKE TANGO PERSONALLY

It's a just matter of the math. Over time, if you stay in tango for any length of time, you'll dance with many men, hundreds of them creeping into thousands given that you attend classes and evenings of tango and it begins to add up. But you don't or won't fall in love with all of them or even some of them and then maybe just two or three if any at all and for a very short time. Why? Well, in some ways, tango is the safest romance on the planet given the risk reward ratio. A few dances with a decent leader are generally what you sign up for. This is not to say that some tango entanglements don't go the distance as evidenced by couples who seem dedicated to each other and then one day show up with an infant in a baby carrier in hand that someone watches over while the couple dances …until the child cries and no amount of surrogate rocking the cradle will do. But there's a natural anecdote to tango romance that ensures love's manifold dramas don't decimate the ranks too much.

Sometimes you see a man across the room and you check out how he dances and you think to yourself: *I must dance with him! He's cool, he leads well, he's handsome, age appropriate and this could be something interesting. This could be a special dance or more but at the least a special dance with the perfect stranger.* Then one crowded or slow night which is to say, there's a shift, you *finally* get to dance with him because he asks you out of the blue. You're thrilled. It could be one of those evenings that people take more risk and go outside their comfort zone or there's a shortage of women or the stars are in rare alignment. And yes, you could have asked *him* but in my early and middle days of tango, I preferred to be asked especially with a man I had my eye on that perhaps other women were also eyeing. In those cases, I simply feel better knowing *he* chose *me.* I need the intentionality. I'm not saying it has any universal merit; I'm just saying that most of the time, that's what works for me.

But guess what? When you slide into the arms of this sought-after contender and the music starts it's instantly awkward or he's weird or there's no dance chemistry and it's just *so* off it's almost painful for both of you. You just couldn't have known this from the outside in. But tango being tango, you can of course figure this out in the *first* few bars of that first dance. But guess what? It's part of a four-dance set but guess again?

You're stuck for three more dismal dances because of the *tanda* rule. What is a *tanda*?

A *tanda* is a set of four tangos or three waltz or three faster-paced milongas. It's a basic politesse of tango to complete the set of dances with the person you are already with. Unlike Salsa or West Coast Swing which features one day with a person where you can *opt* to continue with that person for another round, tango respects a trio or quartet of dances with the same person. However good or bad the *tanda,* you endure the whole of it with a bland and hidden resignation. When a dubious (or simply bad) *tanda* ends you nod to your partner and wander away deliberately slowly so that you don't actually look like you're fleeing (which of course, you are) and when you really want to high-tail off the dance floor. As you make your way to the water fountain or ladies room you think, *well thank goodness that's done! Can you imagine if I had dated him?* You experience the twin feelings of disappointment (dashed hopes, fantasy lost) and relief (*it doesn't have to be him/phew/I dodged a bullet*). While there was no romance and/or it wasn't pleasant it was finite. Things always play out on the dance floor and tango among *all* dances proves this most conclusively. Packaging isn't always a sign of coming attractions; it can also be false advertising or all form and no content but you don't know until you're there. And to quote John Lennon, often, *there's no there, there.*

In the civilian dating world, a lack of chemistry can hold up for two sedate coffee/dinner/movie dates but in tango it's not sustainable beyond the *tanda.* That lack of chemistry is a huge elephant in the room. But on the flip side, I've danced with men who seemed totally out of synch with me (from the outside) and yet unexpectantly had the best dances of all.

But generally if you're either wise or somewhat cool of heart (and/or you'll most likely will become so as time goes on) you'll fall in love with none of your partners or *only* until the set of dances end unless it was something bigger than dance-floor chemistry that got fed over time with conversations, coffee and civilian dating.

Few people *outside* of tango can fathom not falling for each of your partners even in regular dance classes because tango looks so romantic.

No one looking in from outside could possibly believe that the sheer humanity and musical connection we're all after in tango could supersede a romantic one or be at least as important but it's true. This is also how one manages to stay in tango for years because you're not crashing into love affairs that burn out in very short time with any sort of regularity. Not to mention, if it's hard to walk and chew gum at the same time, it's close to impossible to be seduced or seduced as you really need to concentrate. You need to take that stuff off the floor when you're more casually chit-chatting with someone.

Even beginners quickly learn to separate their feelings for the dance and the feelings for the men leading them. You can pretend, flirt or portray some intensity of romantic theatrics but beyond the quartet of dances you don't lose your head or your heart or your steps. Tango is not a one-off; it's a marathon. Plus the more times (different occasions, classes, evenings, days or nights) you dance with the same person the more you get to know them.

Many people would fib about this but given the choice of a million perfect dances with strangers and *one* perfect dance with your soulmate it's no contest because in tango, you want to go the distance. But if the choice is a million perfect dances with strangers or the same million with your soulmate? Well, you know the answer to that too. I suppose what we all really want is both: the perfect strangers and the soulmate dances, i.e. all of it!

This all being said, it would be really uncomfortable if everyone was sussing out everyone like speed dating done to music especially if you want a decent tango life. Tango, and this is a major reality check, takes so much concentration (especially in the beginning) to follow anyone with some aptitude that it would be disastrous to start crushing on each and every person who asks you to dance. You start stumbling or mixing up your steps or stepping on their feet, which is a feat considering you are mostly walking backwards. So you can either devote yourself to the dance or the leader (speaking as a follower) but it's almost impossible to do both although a little of each leaches through a lot of the time. Once you start assessing the man as a *man* in a very personal way instead of as a leader and fellow dancer, you tend to lose your tango ability as proportional to the rise in your subjectivity. When you're already in someone's arms so that's proximity enough.

Tango is like a profession that has its own rules and a code of behavior. As toasty a dance as it can be, it's subtle. *Even* if you think there's something special in the stranger who's asked you to dance, that magic might disappear if you switch to a tango waltz, milonga or simply on another evening, the magic can disappear as if it never was. You might not even *remember* the man nor he you because a lot of tango partners have come down the pipe between one dance set and another. Although, also true is that you not remember a face but you can always remember the trademark feel of their embrace.
There are men I've forgotten until I slip into their arms and think, '*ah yes, this feels familiar; it's…Juan*'.

Like strange weather, there's a mercurial streak in tango: both it and the people in it often change without reason or warning. It and they can be stormy or balmy, steamy or frosty so it's best you keep your own center.

CHAPTER EIGHT

HOW NOT TO FALL IN LOVE WITH YOUR OWN TANGO PARTNER

When I first came to tango, more-experienced tango women warned me about getting involved with one of my more frequent tango partners – say – like a default class partner. I had no particular intentions in this regard at that moment but I thought – *wow – she must be wrong – why not?*

But then one day I did in fact discover why so many people are hedgy about dating their own tango partners. It's a part of my tango narrative that I refer to as 'the fiasco of Jean Marc' which I suppose is a bit of a spoiler but nonetheless it's a tale that deserves sharing from its disarming and charming start.

I first met Jean-Marc during a weekend session on tango waltz. Actually I'd met him two years prior when he showed up in my regular classes. At that time, he always came pre-paired up with a tall, attractive, red-head that I presumed was his both his dance and life companion or at the least what I termed his 'tango wife'.

Increasingly I began to notice that people had tango spouses or regular partners that are platonics, aka relied upon human bookmarks to hedge their bets. Better the devil you know I guess.

Jean-Marc looked like a cross between Antonio Banderas and Gabriel Byrne in their prime although either of those men, at any age, aren't lacking in appeal. Tall and dark-haired with threads of silver, at fifty-five he could have been a mature male model for Chanel cologne or an elite brandy company. Quiet and reserved, wafting class and education, I heard he was the head of cardiac research at a renowned hospital. Once, on a random evening instead of a class one, he asked me to dance. It felt strange because we were hyper aware of each other having been in classes together but fortuitously this time he showed up without his clinging vine. Alas, anti-climatically, our dance connection was laced in uncertainty. It wasn't helped by the fact that we didn't match at all in height, rhythm or dance sensibility but there was just a visceral discomfort. It was a memorable *tanda* but not a positive way. It was unfortunately notable for its awkwardness and I was disappointed.

Sometime later we finally both turned up at another tango studio and *this* time we were paired together as default partners for an eight-week course. Despite a patent lack of romantic interest on his part Jean-Marc always a lot of interesting things to say and he was a good listener.

This time, at least at first, he was a decent enough partner. I maintained a mild interest simply based on the fact that he was pleasant, intelligent, a peer and I'll give him this, he was quite handsome.

Our dancing improved somewhat as I adapted to accommodate him. It's what a good follower does and because I liked him I made a lot of extra effort. Still, he danced far too fast without really listening to the music or me and my shorter legs were no match for his stilts which were prone to quick and unpredictable moves. Sorry to say, dancing with him was a rough ride. One evening, his twenty-one year old son came at the end of the class to watch his father dance. At the next class, Jean Marc told me his son gave him the thumbs up to his dancing and his partner (me). I was chuffed at the endorsement. Maybe this could be something after all and I decided to ignore the inferior dance collaboration. You can't have everything.

On another note, beside the tango venue was a lovely tapas restaurant with a beautiful terrace and stringed lights. I'd often pass the restaurant and observe the happy groups but mostly fixated on the couples enjoying tapas and drinks, laughing and talking late into the spring, summer and early fall evenings. I vowed that one day I too would be with a man I cared for and enjoy sitting on that terrace, chatting and nibbling on plates of baguette rounds, cheeses, fresh figs and honey. That was my go-to rom com visualization – to be part of that portrait of a couple who linger on a summer night at the Spanish bistro after tango class.

After his son's visit that evening something shifted. Jean Marc went from polite and distant to overtly flirtatious! He lit up asking me more personal questions and barraging me with compliments. Somehow, inexplicably I'd graduated from a respectful partner to a possible contender. It was a pleasant but bewildering change especially when he whispered in my ear: *I think about you all the time.* What? How did we go from impersonal civility to this? I cautiously responded to this development wondering: did he suddenly get divorced, had a lobotomy, or was he drunk?

After class he walked me to my car and the following week, he invited me for tapas at the terrace café. Evidently I had segued out of the friend zone and going to the tapas cafe with my attractive tango partner. Hello vision board! Bless the laws of manifestation!

Predictably (for me at least) I began filling out the perfect boyfriend template. Perhaps I was too keen to prioritize form over content but so much about the premise seemed so right – at least on paper. Whatever didn't fit, I just edited out.

Over a feast of tasty tidbits I delighted in having his undivided attention and getting to know him a bit more. Conversation flowed as I learned he wasn't married but separated for eight years. Neither he nor his ex-wife wanted to bother with the expensive legalities and there didn't seem to be any love lost. Somehow I blithely ignored this fact which for a woman who took out a second mortgage to pay for her divorce is saying something. In fact he told me, his estranged wife never spoke to him and had blocked him on email and text. *That nasty woman*, I thought. *He's so nice, that's so undeserved* ! I warmed to him even more. He was impressively bilingual, no trace of English in his French; no trace of French in his English as he gracefully toggled back and forth in both tongues with me and the waitress. He had an easy charm and we riffed from subject to subject, profound and light.

I finally asked him why his behavior had shown such an about-face, *For months, even years, we've been in classes together and you've been really circumspect and it just seems so sudden that you're noticing me – not that there's anything wrong with that but there's been such a change....*

He responded by saying he'd started new prescription for anti-depressants a few weeks prior and suddenly it was like he totally just woke up renewed and found himself smitten. That was nice and told him so but privately I wondered: *if this is a Pfizer-forward romance and his crush is drug-induced then how real can this be?"* Plus I had the distinct feeling had he re-emerged from a moody slumber and found a Dalmatian in tango shoes standing in front of him he would have similarly glommed onto the spotted furry candidate and bestowed the same affections.

As we left the restaurant he shared that he was at the end of a relationship with someone else but there was a planned vacation with another couple. He told me he would feel like a heel not following through. Since I wasn't too invested instead of seeing this as a red flag I thought ok, this is *good; I have time to think, have a week off without him in tango so I can relax and time will tell.* The evening ended and I drove him home. He hesitated as he got out of the car but made no move. I said goodnight and I drove home to my sleeping sons, paid the babysitter, made chamomile tea and watched *The American President* for the umpteenth time.

Two weeks later, Jean-Marc later he announced he was a free man! He had broken up with his person and was ready to go forward. It really had been over a long time, he said, and whisked away my suggestion that perhaps he take some time to himself or he was on the rebound.

This news came with yet more Spanish tidbits at the restaurant, walks and talks and then one night as I was getting out of the car, he pounced. Without any sort of preamble (although in retrospect I guess I missed the clues) there was an onslaught of dramatic kisses and roving hands that were more startling than seductive. Like our tango, and apparently all else about Jean Marc, it wasn't smooth. It could have been the mechanics (there was a lot of velocity and I was exiting the car at the same time) or a patent, notable lack of chemistry because I didn't feel anything. In fact, I felt completely disconnected and like an observer instead of a participant. Still, I agreed to meet him the next night to go to a local olive oil-tasting at restaurant opening.

Once I arrived at his condo I realized the olive oil tasting was off the table because clearly he'd planned a grand seduction. As I entered his dimly lit home he said, *do you really want to go to a silly olive oil tasting?* Actually I did. I wanted to get to know him casually at first or connect more than we had until this point. To me, as a foodie, things like olive-oil tastings are also never silly. His co-opting of the evening wasn't unexpected but I was ambivalent and still determined to get the full experience of a being woo-ed. How poetic was it to take a duet from the dance floor to the bedroom and fulfil tango's murky promise in a fairytale ending that promised an Astor Piazzolla-esque quartet at my autumn wedding?

Well it was indeed murky. On the way to the bedroom he cautioned me that he wasn't 'fully functional' as a result of both the wrong dose and wrong type of anti-depressants that were still being adjusted. There's something to be said for pacing out one's revelations. Nonetheless, I understood completely or so I told him but frankly it's enough to worry about your own self let alone take on someone else's nervousness. Now I was caught between anticipation and reticence which is to say romance flew out the window as ambivalence moved in.

Moreover, for a man who chatted up a good game he approached the whole bedroom experience like a serious mission. He was admirably earnest but everything on his end was highlighted by apologies and self-effacing statements, all of which only served to remind me I could be bidding on EBay or feeding a sourdough starter. Being supportive in that context with a relative stranger does little to encourage libido. In short, it was a travail. It might have been lightened with a sense of ease or humor but Jean-Marc was more the uber-sincere Lothario sort and nothing lightens things less than lots of hang-ups bereft of the balance of some humor.

A week or two later he spoke of role play games we might play, toys and costumes we might fiddle with. *We need to get you a chair* he once mentioned. I cringed and wondered why on earth why we needed a chair? The room had a fair-sized bed; why a chair for goodness sakes? I didn't want to ask and I just hoped he'd forget. Also for me, as a purist in these matters (i.e. it's *who* you're with) this seemed silly plus without the some basic viability in place, what was the difference if I (or he) dressed up as a sexy nurse or not. That said, I am pretty certain he meant for me to wear the costume. I'm not judging his wants and needs only to say that it didn't ring any bells for me especially when the basics weren't quite down or rolling smoothly along.

The weeks unfolded and we did enjoy bookstores, restaurants, artsy music events and movies. There was the huge bonus of always having a tango partner on hand although we continued to dance poorly. As a tactic to counter this, I'd wait until he made a visit to the men's room and then madly seek out other dance partners to sate tango self with. For Jean-Marc's part, he spoke about his preference for dancing with a taller woman so he might feel her cheek against his temple. Had I liked him more or at all (by that point) I might have felt jealous but I was mildly aware that I cared less.

There was also a cultural divide between us for one thing and unfortunately it was one that wasn't brokered by any interest in what I brought to the table. I listened patiently to how his work day unfolded, his career plans for the future and all his past paramours. Conversely he wasn't that interested in my day, career plans or former beaux. But I figured I had other people to share these things if indeed I needed to talk and reasoned you can't have everything in one relationship, totally ignoring the fact that you can indeed insist on some essential equity in any partnership.

There was also the fact that I liked to face life's problems and he talked about letting things stay under a rug. *Why start up,* he often said. He had one adult son who lived on his own whereas I was the head of a family all still under my roof which is to say, I was still awash in responsibilities (like supporting a family of four) and he was foot loose and fancy free. *My ex-wife takes care of my son if something arises* he told me. I compared this to my life at *Animal House* and thought about all the hoops I had to go through as a single mother in order to catapult myself out of my house just to go on a date.

He mused about being a tango gigolo in his next life. I asked him why. *Because I think I'm naturally good with women and feel I could be of service.* Interesting, I said to him with a bland smile. But inside I wanted to exclaim: a *tango gigolo? Are you serious? You are incredibly inconsiderate and ego-centric and a terrible tango partner to boot. How could you come up with this as a possible vocation in any lifetime?*

Another day, another dance he said, *you know, you could have any guy, certainly any man at tango but for one thing. You're too low-maintenance.*

What? I'm sorry – what did you say?

You're too low maintenance. You're lovely and gracious but you're not complicated and you're too reasonable. Men like a challenge.

Inside I thought: *a) first of all, what 'men' are you referring to since I thought I was with you or are you my romance agent? b) you're a full-out arse with mother issues c) men that want artificially 'high maintenance' women are boys with an appetite for drama versus connection.* Again, I smiled benignly and on the outside, the person known as 'polite me' said *thank you, duly noted.*

We argued a lot which for a newish relationship is never a good sign. To be fair, I guess he wanted something and I wanted something or something else and neither of us were the right thing for each other. But we both held on nonetheless because there was a certain logic to it all (we were both intelligent, educated, reasonable people and peers) but that's not what makes things work at a visceral level.

With Jean-Marc I began to appreciate that I was an adult woman – not a girl. I was both holding down a household and raising three young men all alone. By contrast, the man I was dating and dancing with seemed spoiled and immature and I resented being stronger and more grounded. I don't have to be rescued or always 'be the girl' but I do need an equal.

He also mentioned his wealth several times and his highly regarded position at the research institute and compared this to me – essentially single mother, freelance writer and remarked how badly he felt for me that I was so stressed. It *sounded* kindly but I think there was a power dynamic that characterized everything. He spoke about gifts I might like but he never bought or gave them. On a late Saturday afternoon, we went to a trendy imported clothing boutique in his neighborhood and he asked me to pick out outfits I might like and then nodded to the saleswoman and we left without so much as a scarf. I had no expectations of any sort of gifts but I don't understand what the outing was all about altogether.

Once he said I deserved a spa weekend to simply relax which again, seemed generous. But in my mind I envisioned his suitcases full of toys, costumes (and that chair) and extra batteries and realized it would hardly be relaxing nor a gift or certainly not a gift for *me* which I guess was the whole point.

On another occasion, we went to a café and he flirted with an openly gay woman who must have thought he was daft and I just thought: well, *seriously – this is uncool.* But again, no tell-tale jealousy.

Over the next few weeks, things kept spiraling until one evening at an Italian restaurant he said he had a terrible headache.

Apparently, he confessed, *just* talking to me gave him a headache and on the drive home he said *let's finish this; it's not working.*

I was both insulted and relieved but before I could say anything he said*: Also tomorrow night is tango class. I feel badly because you won't have a partner since I won't dance with you. So that you don't lose your tango class money, how about I give you $50 to make up for it?*" Of course I declined thinking, there's simply not enough medication or money to make this outrageous man at a nice or classy person.

The next night I went to the class and fortunately there was an extra leader for me. I avoided Jean-Marc like the plague and the instant replacement he'd found - a statuesque blond woman who cracked gum through the class like Siegfried and Roy snapping a whip at the lions.

I never ever spoke to Jean Marc afterwards and if we saw each other on occasion, I walked past and through him like he was a ghost. Brava - I was finally high maintenance.

About 18 months later I got an email from him: *I've always felt badly about the abrupt and harsh way I parted company with you. Would you like to have coffee and talk?* I never answered because *how* he parted company was the least of it. I'm generally prone to being forgiving but conversely adept at sniffing out dubious intentions. I decided that silence was the most eloquent response.

After that, I never, ever again saw Jean-Marc at tango or anywhere else.

The gift of Jean-Marc however which served me both in and outside tango was that romantic is as romantic does. That reality cured me of being fooled by packaging or my own longings that had a tendency to put a veil on reality. Lots of tango men look like the stuff of your girlish dreams - at least from a distance: the distance between the thirty feet across the dance floor. Up close and personal, they often simply aren't. They are just people.

There's also that saying that tango is a vertical expression of a horizontal desire. But trust me, whatever isn't working in tango's vertical world probably won't work any better in life's horizontal one.

CHAPTER NINE

THE DAIRY QUEEN TANGO MEETS LORD OF THE DANCE

I could have danced all night
I could have spread my wings
And done a thousand things
I've never done before.
I'll never know
What made it so exciting;
Why all at once
My heart took flight.

From My Fair Lady
Frederick Lowe, Alan Jay Lerner

As I look out my window I can see it's not quite winter but not clearly spring which means it must be around St. Patrick's Da. This is my cue to head to the kitchen to bake batches of homey, rustic soda bread which is one of my favorite things to bake. It's also on occasion that makes me recall, and with much pleasure, my most memorable St. Pat's Day.

A few years ago, as the March 17th holiday approached I happened to mention to a few tango friends that I was making soda breads as gifts for friends and family. Most of my tango-mates had never heard of soda Bread and I was happy explained my pet recipe.

On hearing this, my default class partner at the time, Paul, perked up and began to wax lyrical about soda breads. Here was this part French, part Italian, Argentine wanna-be, ultra-macho tanguero that knew about soda breads! So few people do. He was more than a fan; he was a soda bread addict. I was so surprised and finding it charming I thought, *perhaps I will surprise Paul next week with freshly baked soda bread,* I thought.

As the following week's class began however, Paul, a rather good dancer albeit a perfectionist, was in a darker mood of a spectrum of his moody states. He became increasingly annoyed as another tango leader kept up his habit of looking at his own feet as he led his partner. Consequently and with remarkable consistency he bumped (hard!) into everyone on the dance floor which of course is bound to occur if you're not navigating properly and/or looking down at your feet. The shoe-gazer, the perennially downcast Christian was generally a nice person but became e a virtual terror on a crowded dance floor. That evening, head bowed as he led his partner around the dance perimeter, he did his bumper car routine once too many times for Paul's tolerance. Around the third bump and nudge incident, without any warning, Paul suddenly hauled off and neatly pushed-almost-slugged the other man, dragging me with him in one clean sweep! Unbelievable! It caused Christian and his partner, Giselle to totter and they almost fell over as did I. Other dance couples leaped in to help them avoid hitting the floor. I was aghast – and caught between apologizing to the other couple while somehow maintaining a modicum of loyalty to my own partner who had also threw me off my own balance. Everyone who witnessed it was shocked. Tango *is* a contact sport but it generally does not involve full body checking. The tense moment was gotten past, but not without sulky angry looks the rest of the night, incredulity from everyone else, and the occasional snarling comments from the two men as we two couples danced by each other.

Well, I thought – *forget about the soda bread plan! That man does not deserve soda bread. How uncivilized, how gauche!* I am nothing if not allergic to temper. But as the week went on, I mellowed. Soda bread wouldn't be such a bad thing; stuff happens, feelings settle. Maybe it is *Pulp Fiction*/tango guy stuff.

So for the next tango class, I relented. I baked and brought a beautiful soda bread along with me, still warm from the oven, perched on its baking sheet. I gave it to Paul as soon as I arrived. He actually teared up. Now *that* is the power of the Irish baking. I was pleased after all I had decided to make it after all rather than withhold the gift. The better road was the higher road and Paul's undisguised pleasure and appreciation was my reward.

The mercifully uneventful tango class ended and feeling the winter-ending, spring-on-its-way dusky air, I decided it was post-tango *Dairy Queen* night. In fact, the DQ had opened just that day for the new season. It was an evening that called for hot chocolate fudge sundae with raspberries. Paul asked to tag along.

We sat in the *Dairy Queen* at the indoor café tables, the only people in the place, and we chatted about tango over ice cream and chunks of soda bread. Paul, remarking on the newly laid marble floor in the *Dairy Queen* terrace where we sat – now empty of patrons except the two of us. I thought nothing of his observation – tango people are always looking at floors and considering their dance worthiness.

Then all too soon, the lights began to dim, and the young man who had served us, now began his rituals of closing up the shop and stacking the café chairs on the tables. I reached for my coat and my purse. Just as we were just about to leave, and only a few ambience lights were left on, spattering out tiny sprays of light on that marble floor, Paul asked for my coat and purse. Perplexed, I handed him my things which he cavalierly threw over a chair back. He beckoned in one gesture, drew me into his arms, and hummed a familiar *Gardel* tune, struck a dramatic pose and then whisked me away. We swirled, dipped, ducked and tripped the light fantastic to the awestruck stare of the young man, the Dairy Queen employee, who simply leaned on his mop and watched us tango.

"I told you this was a great floor to dance on', Paul smiled into my hair, as we covered at least more one mini acre, causing our audience of one to widen his eyes into pure astonishment.

Somebody pinch me, I thought. *My life just became a movie.*

Best yet, it was one of those times where I followed seamlessly. I hadn't time to protest, resist or otherwise balk or become self-conscious and second guess my moves. Everything just flowed.

When the inner music ended, we stayed in one of those hovering tango poses and then we simply dissolved, the outlines of our bodies dispersing again into the air and atmosphere. We left the shadow version of us, lingering in our own reality wake. For a moment there was only the sound of the ice-cream compressors who hummed their ovation.

Coat and purse were handed back to me and we waved goodbye to the gaping young man and his mop partner. Into the lamp-lit street we went, where the mist from the pavement was joined by the teasing feathers of a lightly falling snow. As if central casting had requested it, there was a full moon, gleaming on this magical night of good luck. I could almost hear the dim music of Michael Flatly *Lord of the Dance* in my imagination thought I saw an impish leprechaun tango down the black and shiny, wet street.

We soon parted as Paul walked his own way as his home was nearby and I went to my car. As each snowflake melted on my face, it occurred to me how many perfect conversations take place without a word ever being spoken. It's always a good policy to judge less and bake more. There but for the grace of a little forgiveness and warm Irish soda bread, fragrant of dusty wholemeal wheat and sweet Thompson raisins I might never have had that experience on a mellow March night. Instead my evening might have ended with a solo chicken wrap ejected from the window of McDonald's drive-thru. I also attribute this interlude to the moonlight, spring fever, and what a little tango magic can do. Perhaps it is in part also due to Paul who was difficult but at least on that particular March 17th, a perfect match-up.

Btw I haven't seen Paul in the longest while. For years he told me the notion of getting married and worse, the very idea having kids made him nauseous. He was around fifty years old when he told me that. One day a lean-and-mean, twenty-five year old medical student came to tango. She spotted Paul was immediately smitten even as he protested her attentions many times over. However she was persistent, got her man and eventually they married. I heard they since had a child or two. Sometimes, while his wife was working at the hospital Paul came to tango alone but then one day, he disappeared altogether.

What was surprising was a) he was adamant about marriage and domestic life and b) he was devoted to tango and now he was MIA. In some ways he's the reverse of me – I was married with three kids and found tango and a bit of less-domesticate pathways Conversely, he was a non-conformist to begin with and then settled down or perhaps not – but he's nowhere to be found and trust me I've checked every Dairy Queen.

Here's my recipe for my famous *Lord of the Dance Tango Irish Soda Bread.*

Tango Class Irish Soda Bread or Lord of the Dance Soda Bread

Clabber is an old fashioned word for buttermilk. This makes a majestic soda bread that is great with cheese or sliced cold corned beef.

3 cups whole-wheat flour
3 cups all-purpose flour
1/2 cup brown sugar, firmly packed
2 teaspoons baking powder
2 teaspoons baking soda
1 ½ teaspoons salt
1/2 cup very cold, unsalted butter, diced
2 cups buttermilk
1 cup dark raisins, plumped and dried

Finishing Touches

Bran or fine oatmeal, for dusting

Preheat the oven to 425 F. Stack two baking sheets together and line the top one with parchment paper.

In a large food processor briefly blend the flours, sugar, baking powder, baking soda, and salt. Add in the butter and pulse until the mixture is grainy.

Remove to a large mixing bowl and make a well in the center. Stir in the buttermilk with a fork, gathering dough together. When almost mixed fold in the raisins. Dough will be still somewhat ragged.

Turn out onto a lightly floured work surface and knead gently to make a firm dough, using a little additional flour on your board to help firm up if the dough is too wet.

Let rest 5 minutes and then shape dough into a large round and place on baking sheet. Make a cross with a knife, and dust with bran or fine oatmeal.

Bake until done and soda breads are nicely browned all over, about 35-45 minutes.

Makes 1 large bread

INTERLUDE

MILONGAS AND PRACTICAS

I've mentioned the concept of the *tanda* before but a little expansion on the subject might be in order. Aside from dancing three to four songs with one person in a set, a *tanda* is generally songs of the same type. There are a few types of music under the umbrella of Argentine Tango, being regular or traditional *tango*, *vals* or waltz tango, and *milonga* which is a faster and definitely upbeat tango. A *tanda* can be comprised of all traditional tangos, or all vals or all milongas. The *tanda* may also be comprised of a grouping of music by the same composer or in the same style or era so you can get into a certain dance groove and this is at the discretion of a talented tango DJ.

Leaders often wait to hear the type and style of music before deciding to dance and selecting a partner. This happens very quickly but it certainly occurs. Tango is nothing if not about strategizing.

Generally, when a couple has agreed to dance we complete the *tanda* with that person. It's bad form *not* to complete the *tanda* and I've rarely seen that done and only have done that once myself. On that occasion, the partner in question kept going on his hands and knees and with his two hands, forcefully moving my feet this way or that to 'show' me what he wanted. Understandably, I walked off the dance floor and far away from him!

As a rule, we don't quit mid-*tanda* because of the person's dancing style or lack of skill. Aside from my extreme experience above, there are rare times people break the dance set because of the rudeness of a partner or basic incompatibility. Generally you soldier on. The only real reason for abandoning ship is because feel unsafe (you've been navigated into furniture or other couples), you're being embraced in an uncomfortable way or perhaps your shoe strap broke but it's generally at your discretion. Discomforts such as sore ankles, sweatiness, and too much perfume or after shave are dealt with –but of course, a broken or loose shoe strap does call for a pause and intervention.

More explanations: *The* Milonga or *A* Milonga

In the world of tango, the word *milonga* also has two meanings. *Milonga* can refer to a briskly-paced tango for which the music is characteristically brisk, rhythmical and upbeat. You can simply tell by the very first few bars that 'it's a *milonga* and the energy on the dance floor suddenly shifts as some dancers depart the floor (they don't enjoy *milongas* or don't yet know how to dance them) and others start teeming with energy and gear up. *Milongas* are a happy tango and you feel it in an instant! In fact, they are so joyous that even as they are officially 'tangos', they can give a salsa a run for its money.

As with *vals* or waltz tangos, at least three *milongas* of these jollier, looser-danced tunes are played in a set which makes for happy but sweaty dancers. When you say *yes* to someone on the verge of *tanda* of *milongas* be forewarned: you're committing to three fast-paced dances so be prepared and fasten your seatbelt. This is also because each *milonga* tends to be faster than the one that preceded it so you're in for a penny and in for a pound.

The ***second*** meaning of the word *milonga* simply means a soirée or dance evening.

A *milonga* can be held in the daytime, especially in summer or early evening, outside in parks in cities that have enough tango to offer tango a fresco. But most often, *milongas* take place at night, generally starting at 9 pm and going on until midnight or as late as two or four in the morning. At a *milonga*, you'll meet people from your tango classes especially if it's a *milonga* attached to the dance studio you attend.

Comparable to a *milonga* is the less formal, *practica* or the practice occasions that most dance schools offer, setting aside time and space to allow their students to hone up what they've learned. Here you can attend a more relaxed atmosphere and encounter fellow students and teacher. It's an ideal opportunity to brush up on some steps you've done in class or just dance in a more casual atmosphere as well as socialize. You can also expect to meet new people, tango strangers as it were, which in tango, are not really strangers at all. After all, you all 'speak tango' and anyone, familiar or new can end up being your next best tango partner. Over time, these times can blur into a whirlwind of dances and partners but some stand out.

Milonga One

It was the last milonga of winter, an end-of-winter tango event in *the Winter of My Tango Discontent*. Actually, I was in a dual tango *and* life funk. I was in one of my cobwebby states and in a nutshell, I was hardly in the mood to pick up my heels and run to tango. But I also always have believed that anything physical, even mediocre tango that I'm *not* in the mood for is still a good thing.

It was nice to see that other world again where people were all dressed up. I wore a black halter top with a matching shrug and a black, lilac and deep purple tulle skirt which offered a lovely lovely flow and twirl for very little movement on my part. Note to self: always wear something you're comfortable in but also makes you feel like a million bucks and adds a sense of grace. It picks you up from the outside in.

During the course of the evening, it turned out it was Jose, one of the tango teacher's birthdays. Jose is about forty years old and has the blackest, shiniest hair ever that flows to his waist, down his back, in a pony tail of diminishing proportions. It starts like a pony's tail and by the end of its journey down his spine it's as narrow as a piece of shoestring black licorice. Overall, Jose is a wild thing like some feral being you coaxed inside from a dusty, Latin frontier into civilization for one evening. He only adds to this impression because he also does Flamenco complete with whips, foot stomping *and* in addition, he plays tango on his fiddle, strutting the floor as he does so.

That night I discovered that tango has a tradition extended to birthdays of its community who are in attendance on their day, at tango. At some point in the evening everyone forms a circle around the dance floor and the birthday boy (or girl), at this event, it was Jose, enjoys a few tangoes with a string of women who keep cutting in on each other to take a twirl with the special guest. It's a beautifully choreographed hand-off and it's done with such genuine grace in both directions – both Jose leading each new woman and with each new woman in turn, uplifting him with her presence. Each partner Jose danced with danced with and for him but also in a subtle but competitive way for the crowd to show what she can do different or better than her predecessor.

This was the first time I experienced this tradition. I was too shy to dance with Jose in the best of times, let alone within the circle of tango spectators. But then I felt a nudge from a fellow who I knew, and one of my best all time partners. He's short and stalky and while his English is fluent and fluid there's a Latin inflexion to his words. He's proudly told me on several occasions that he's Ecuadorian. He shows up in my tango class most times as an 'extra' or what I call the *tango gigolos.* Marco is, simply so easy-going, caring, elegant, subtle and able to receive or 'hear' his female partners so that a dance with him is pure pleasure. After the nudge which did get me to dance with Jose, I danced two tandas with Marco until we released each other to dance with others. As it was then nearing midnight (and my babysitter was only good until 1:00 am) I had to leave. Out of the corner of my eye I caught another tried-and-true partner, Lucien.

Lucien was at the end of the room, hanging on the edges looking a bit dour and I wondered if part of it was we never got to dance together although my intention was there. But that's just how it goes: sometimes you prefer to dance with only a couple of favorite someones and you don't always get to dance with all the usual suspects on your dance card if it's a busy night. Some nights, it's as arid as a desert, insofar as dance cards go but not that night. So, that might explain Lucien's cranky look but the truth also is that I get uncomfortable with Lucien as he has a tendency on occasion to overstep the dance and romance me instead. Romancing someone within the parameters of the dance isn't as romantic as it seems. For instance, Lucien gets so engrossed that he crosses over from expressive to Oscar-winning dramatic. In doing so, he loses his ability to lead, not to mention I feel pressured as each movement and gesture begins to take on more significance and Lucien gazes into my eyes, as we're moving, with a piercing question in them. More than once I've sensed him measuring my 'person' or female/woman response *versus* responding to the response of my steps as his follower.

In my beginner days these things felt flattering but now they only compromise the magic and the ease of the dance. So I carefully skirted around Lucien as I left lest I ignite any turbulence but sometimes there's just no tonic.

As I got towards the coat room I saw a new fellow who had come barely twenty minutes before and yet he too was leaving. I knew he had not danced at all and asked him, *are you leaving without one dance?"*

He replied, *there's no one to dance with.* The subtext of this is he might not have seen a class partner or someone familiar or simply someone approachable and was retreating. I was still in a pseudo confident haze, fresh from the dance floor, relaxed and warmed up (aka replete) and I guess I felt generous or at least confident. True I was heading home and already dreaming of drive-thru ice-coffee somewhere but any additional interludes or dances would be a bonus that one couldn't pass on.

I told him: *you can dance with me for one tanda you like. I'm leaving soon but no one should come out to tango and go home without having danced.*

He agreed, doffed his coat, put on his shoes and off we went.

He was a lavish dancer, a bit rocky but energetic, generous and a risk-taker. I rather like that type of speed if there's flow. During the second dance he whispered in my ear, while patting his heart, saying that he couldn't believe his luck in finding someone to begin with and someone so good to dance with. We ended with a Montreal kiss on each cheek. I let him know that I'm sometimes there at practice sessions or perhaps we'd bump into each other again at some point and then I made my excuses to leave. As I got on my coat I turned and noticed him murmuring more sweet nothings into a new tango contender. There he was, patting his heart again and murmuring the same sweet nothings. And so it goes I thought, and I smiled.

With a nod bonsoir to a few people I knew I headed out into the chilly night, the streets now gleaming with the residue of a light November snow that had melted leaving a shiny black surface as glossy as the patina on new tango shoes. Once in my car I reached for the pink patterned thermos I got in Chinatown the summer before, knowing then it would come in handy at a time like this. It was full to the brim with hot blackberry tea and honey. I sipped, kicked off my tango shoes, started the car, turned on the calm of a Chopin play-list and started my way home.

To me, when we live in a world in which there's tango which is legal, social in the best of ways, topped off with music and a bit of mystery, it's unfathomable to me that people consider dubious, often illegal, mind-altering substances. There's perfection to be had – unpredictable, connective, energizing: perfection from dance. Dance is a drug but one with little downside so it's fair to say it balances out the addictive qualities.

Milonga Two
Alain the Columbian at Moka Danse Drop In Class

The other night I paid a visit to one of those drop-in tango classes at a place called **Moka Danse**. It's a place where you can just show up at 8 pm, find a random partner and take the informal house class (which is usually a somewhat more advanced level) that lasts an hour. At 9 pm, the class ends, the lights dim, and the music changes to more sultry tangos. It takes a few minutes for the remnant dancers to leave the dance class floor and transition to a soiree. Essentially it's a milonga open to those who have already attended the class as well as those who show up a bit later for the evening.

What is especially serendipitous about these drop-in classes is that remarkably there's always just the right ratio of men to women or the perfect amount of leaders to followers. On an odd occasion there's one more man or one extra woman but even then a couple of minutes pass, the class starts and inevitably a man or woman strolls in a bit late and the ratio of men to women is once again equal. Either gender is often able to dance the part of lead or follower so anyone who strolls in can even things out.

The atmosphere is more casual at these drop-in tango classes because the risk factor is less insofar as you generally think to go at the last minute and you take your chances that there will be a partner and the instruction will be helpful or fun. These classes tend to be filled with newbies (hopeful and happy) and veterans (calm and easy going about it all) and it's a good mix. The focus of the class itself ranges from doing a combination of things or one complex step no one ever seems able to master. But it's always upbeat, often hard work and the ambience, at least for me, is perfect. I generally luck out and find someone I know or someone new. Either way, it's always a different experience and always for various reasons, a good one. But last night was particularly special.

After the class ended last night, I noticed there was an unusual ratio of extra men who had showed up for the evening of dance. The atmosphere was a bit tense because it was a rare situation where there were very few women to dance with. I was scooped up by a man that I'd never seen before, a 30-ish fellow who told me his name was Alain and that he was from Columbia. He was about 5' 9 ", brawny but surprisingly quick and nimble for someone so athletic of build. He had long glossy black hair, tethered back in a ponytail and wore a heavy Aran Irish sweater which struck me as odd because what could be more hot to dance in! He wafted cloud of *Armani's Aqua di Gorgio* and that scent with the wooly sweater and a touch of sweat was like being enfolded in male sunshine. Turned out he was also a strategic and smart dancer.

Some men go over and over the same step, never mixing it up with anything else until you're a robot, and anticipating the lead without being led - but not this guy. He never repeated a single step or combination twice. He had the optimal embrace and the warmth of his personality wafted over into his dance style. A person's body but more so their embrace is their calling card; it's a physical manifestation of how, who and what they are. Even though this man was relatively young, he was confident and had that Latin to-the-manner-born-tango in his DNA. I don't think I ever felt that received or welcomed in a long time. Even a day later, I'm tired, busy with work and yet still thinking of a man I am not attracted to but can remember every inch of him and how well we danced. He was just that right balance of smooth and sometimes syncopated and that wonderful amalgam of gentle, strong, and directed. He danced all over the map: fast, slow, transitions of directions, changes in levels, turns, twists, pauses and then tiny, subtle nuanced things. This in turn brought out the best in me and all different versions of me and yet each one is still essentially me. Like some men instinctively know how to kiss, this man knew how to lead tango.

For the standards tangoes, he was polite and capable. The *Nuevo* tangos? He suddenly became as quick as a lion on the hunt: tense, stilted and then another approach entirely as he broadened out his steps, creating choreography in the moment to longer stretches of melody. In the *vals* tango, he was as graceful as a ballroom courtier and in the traditional *milongas*, he was rhythmic and dynamic. This is the triumvirate: interpretation, innovation and attentiveness. Sometimes he approached dramatic but just held back enough to stop us from become a tango cliché.

Not only did this man move he also knew the value of standing still. He took artful breathers at times while the music played or created pauses or crafted hesitations to resonate with the music and the mood, assessing both before setting forth. To me, this is the tango equivalent of meeting someone else's eyes and not talking. This is that sacred intimacy of being present with another human being and it's especially impactful when it's with a total stranger. It's as if you find the one person on the planet that speaks not only your obscure language but its particular dialect. In short, you find your tribe.

Step by step, dance by dance, he tried different steps to see if I could follow and what he could do and what might work successfully as partnering choices so that we eventually had a consensus of dance and were a team. As the music ended his girlfriend or tango 'wife' (aka platonic tango friend) came to claim him. I bid him thanks and he made a small bow and I smiled as I handed him off.

Connections like that are a physical manifestation of your own spirit – that quiet, essential thing inside you that's your emotional home that sometimes you invite a stranger into. In the case of a man who leads a woman in tango that home is where you greet her. You open your arms and your embrace is the entranceway and you choose how wide to open it. If you want to have a great dance, you are expansive with your embrace because that's what allows you to be vulnerable, expressive and known and those are the gateway tools to that craved connection. Tango, like life, is really about being seen for who you are by someone else you also see.

When a body moves, it's the most revealing thing. Dance for a minute, and I'll tell you who you are.

Mikhail Baryshnikov

Another tango dancer once told me, that a man brings his soul to tango whether he wants to or not. This same man also told me, *we all bring all of what we are however grand or however minimalist, to all else we do in life but it's just so apparent in tango.* One can't neither hide a largesse of soul any more than we can inflate a narrow one. That first few seconds of the initial embrace says pretty well all you need to know about who you're dancing with. But this is only if you are paying attention and you have to listen with all five senses as well as your intuition providing yours is operational.

There weren't too many people at this *milonga* and there's no rhyme or reason for it but the given the shortage of women dancers induced the men who don't usually do so to ask me to dance. Shortages in tango real estate do much to inflate property values of the women who are present as they chronically do for the men at most other times. Overall, it was a superb night of dancing. I'm grateful for nights like that. It resets my inner compass and it reminds me to never, ever settle and always make room for the unexpected.

SHALL WE DANCE?

The most beautiful three words in the language I know
Are not,
I love you.
They are, instead -
Shall we dance?

Someone asks you to dance
You say yes –
Your feet grow wings -
Your heart flutters
And you enter the kingdom
Of someone else's arms,
Someone else's tutelage.
You have to let go
You *must* let go
And let them lead.
You have no say -
For the moment you said *yes*

You signed a contract
With your spirit and with theirs.
And now there's no quitting
Until the dance is done.
Or two, or three -
Or perhaps countless dances
Of unthinkable grace,
Until and when
He leads you back -
To where the others sit,
On those spare and rickety café chairs
Where the perfume mingles in fumes
Of small hunger, lesser fear and tempered hope.
You are no longer the same.
You are come back but are never really returned,
All because someone said:
Shall we dance?

CHAPTER TEN

LITTLE DANCE, BIG HEARTBREAK

I'm beginning to think that most people come to tango with an unspoken reason and it's often the same unvoiced reason. That silent subtext seems to be about a heart break, the pure and simple kind that's old-fashioned and sharp or the quiet and relentless sort that puddles along like an inflamed appendix. Heart break seems to be the invisible *Plus One* at your first tango foray until it morphs, which it can and will, but that's only later on.

Certainly, there are people at tango that just want to try out the dance either on its own because they're curious or with significant other or platonic friend and there isn't any accompanying sorrow. But as an observer of the human spirit, I've sniffed out more than a few tales of little or greater heartache, my own included. It can be a new wound or long-standing, faded-to-a-chronic ache but either way, welcome to this clearing house of healing hearts, aka the tango dance floor. Of course, I'm not speaking of couples or come clearly smitten with each other and want to find out about tango – it's mostly the unattached.

From the outside, tango can appear as just a social activity, the proverbial learning a new life skill but tango involves music, people, and being held by someone or holding someone. There's no disguising the appeal of the latter to someone who's in a lost love state because admit it, lawn-bowling it's not.

At any rate the heart wound might be neatly tucked beneath the clothes, in that friendly but cool look in the eyes and non-committal, just-for-strangers smile. Even if it's not just-lost-your-soulmate heart break, there's pain or some loss or if it is past the first stage of those, it could have already transmuted to good, old-fashioned loneliness. It will all reveal over time to the person you're dancing with. Between those precise steps and changes of shoes, in missed beats and word slips, inevitably, a half-story, with half- truths told haltingly and with many interruptions, emerges. Even if one said nothing, the body doesn't lie and you can feel the vibrations. Some people come to tango on a mission. They could be in the just-get-out-there phase or making up for lost times or the deals they cut with the partner that is no longer with them or decided it's life make-over time and mid-life catch-up. Trust me, some big shift is what gets them to the dance floor in a weird part of town, on an evening most people are home watching *Netflix*. You can feel their energy or the hyper cadence of their patter. If I was more generous or less dramatic I would say there are *reasons* versus *seasons* that bring people to tango. The latter could be the season of rediscovering your mate, or your own love of dance or simply remembering yourself.

But if it's for reasons of the heart and a tender one at that, why would *anyone* in this vulnerable state, come to tango? Because there at tango, in someone else's unknowing, unjudgmental arms, is the possibility of exorcism of this heartache.

There's also a contingent of people who are simply solo. Maybe they figure: *I always liked to dance and maybe, perhaps, maybe....I will meet someone at tango.* But that also generally means they've been on their own quite a while and are primed for tango. The heartbreak in those cases was long ago and far away or perhaps it is simply loneliness, which is protracted heartache which segues to garden variety loneliness. Ah loneliness.... the word and the state we try so hard to banish, albeit a part of the human condition, and the one that we carry with such shame.

I think we heartbroken gravitate to what we think is tango's offering in the imagined promised land of seduction. Isn't tango what the billboard advertised: romance, heat and passion? We're not drawn to tango because sushi or knitting class was full nor do we believe tango is where we will meet our new platonic friend. We go because what we think what we lost might be found there. We go because that part of us no one has yet seen or honored, that unique part we fear might not be there after all might reveal in the safe place of *Astor Pizzaolla's Oblivion.*

What I really like about the bobbing tango tales of woe, as they move about the dance is that you while it might be so many people's back story they don't wear it on their sleeve. This should immediately alert you to how sanguine tango people are, even before they really morph *into* tango people. They are poised and sedate with their emotions and let the dance do its work or more to the point, to do the dance, you have to work at it and for ninety minutes, your personal drama becomes the understudy, not the star. So you're free to re-inherit your pride and anonymity of person-hood and in fact, are once again, just a civilian, learning tango. Now cast in the great sea of tango it no longer really matters who you are or who you were and what brought you in the first place. It's a whole new you in a whole new land. You don't need any paperwork for this rite of passage and you can even throw that old identity behind. Save the stories of that for the third date disclosure in your outside life.

At any rate, that old identity begins to feel like a mask or misguided shield you wore so as to pass as normal. At tango, that old and repeated story about you and how you came to tango just proves bulky and you soon find that such armour has no place or weight. Over time, you just stop referring to it at all. The threads are so long unravelled you cannot gather them back up and replay them anyway. Such many new threads are now overlaid and you've transitioned to something else without even knowing it or when it happened. In time, you are dancing, and living and doing so in the present.

One day, at some tango class or tango soirée you stop counting memories and instead you count steps and bars of music and sometimes you even relax. Which means at some point, without thinking too much about it you share your heartache or you listen to someone sharing theirs but at that point, it's a dull ache you barely feel. And the nicest part about it is, in telling it, there, in someone else's arms, them leading you or them holding you, it begins to fade. It begins not to matter how you came to this strange dark world with its lightness of being and generous, human heart. It no longer carries disproportional heft in the *Story of You.* Instead, it becomes just one of the *many* stories of you and one that isn't permanently bookmarked at that particular page.

Is tango romantic? Of course it is. But to start with, tango is open-armed. Tango kindly whispers, 'Come *to me with your stories of he-done-you-wrong and she-left-you-again. Instead, we will dance. I will find you an imperfect, perfect stranger who appreciates you for all he/she didn't see'.* In that stranger's arms, sporting their *own* wounds, you find you hear a new music that surprisingly, as foreign as it is you can move to it and it begins to sound as familiar as the chirp of a homing pigeon. Soon, you rediscover that you are once again pretty or handsome or charming or interesting but for certain: you are no longer forgotten or unseen. Your specialness that heartbreak efficiently mangled or that lack-of-acknowledgement that did the same now re-blooms in sweet, gulping little gasps and sighs. Is tango sexy? If gratitude is an aphrodisiac, then yes, tango is sexy.

But then, on the other side of that generosity, tango does take up the seduction slack. It owns your soul and is loath to toss you back to the lovers you might have given a second glance. But now you don't. Because now you have a lover that won't quit. True, this lover only sometimes gives back whilst keeping you for itself, but it also never leaves you. *That* is something; in a world that changes music and dances every other day – that is something.

All those heart wounds you don't see, are there, healing, bar by bar, beat by beat. Any given place, in any city, on any given night, you will see men and women gliding on a dance floor in shadows and echoes until they are as thin as smoke from a fire far and long away, disappearing in the air. All you feel is the residual heat but cannot seem to remember where it came from to begin with. There is no more beginning, middle and end; there's just one long sinew of soul's homecoming.

By the time you do meet someone outside tango or on the dance floor you can barely remember the mini or major angst that first drew you to the dance. You are in fact a whole new animal in another sort of jungle. The stakes have changed, your spirit is transformed and now we have something entirely different to contend with. And whether that new romance goes the distance or not these new citizens stay the course. They fall in love once again but with a whole new world and the big plus is: this is a romance that has no ending on its horizon.

INTERLUDE

TANGO FIRE OR A POIGNANT MOMENT THAT CRUSHED MY HEART FOR REASONS I CAN'T FATHOM

It's difficult for me to attend almost any dance performance including the *Nutcracker Suite* which I attend most years during the holidays because as with most dancers it's almost impossible to be just a spectator. When I watch any performance, I want to be dancing myself! Not that I am at performance level but if you dance, *watching* dance without craving to dance yourself is a challenge. It almost hurts to be still in your seat, see the dancers, what with live music besides. *Always be closing* is the real estate agent credo and always *be dancing* is the dancer's code. But even as a spectator, seeing the troupe *Tango Fire* perform some time ago was so bewitching I forgot I wasn't dancing myself this time and was totally riveted.

You can catch some videos of **Tango Fire** on YouTube and I hope they visit your city one day because they are entertainers who are indescribably magnetic! What I especially liked in the performance I saw that in addition to the troop of sublime dancers, each couple so in synch, the tango musicians were on the stage with the dancers versus being in the orchestra pit. They were seated on a raised platform behind the dancers and were an integral part of the performance. The show was beyond electrifying. It was a confection in music, artistry and entertainment that is tattooed in my memory. But the best part was this: after many standing ovations, too many to count one of the women tango dancers left the side of her performance dance partner and casually strolled over to the violinist seated with the musicians. She gestured to him an invitation to dance, her signalling was very clear to the audience since we certainly couldn't hear her speak. It appeared to be an impromptu move since judging from the reactions of her dance and musician colleagues, there was a bit of a surprise and I had the impression she had impulsively broken rank. What was going on?

After some hesitation, the musician reluctantly put down his violin and the dancer brought him to the middle of the stage.

The ovation quieted and the musicians that were left seated began to play a quiet tango melody which was more of a prompt than an accompaniment.

The man/musician stood in front of the woman, in dance-ready position and quietly removed his glasses and put them in his pocket. The woman raised her shoulders and lifted her arms upwards; the musician created the embrace she then slid into. As if he had all the time in the world and no one else was there, he paused when he first took her in his arms as if he was centering himself and he waited. Then he slowly took flight in gentle, slow but certain steps. The woman, a professional performer, surrendered her stage persona and dancer expertise and was just a woman, dancing with a man, following his lead.

Now dancing instead of playing tango music, surprisingly, the musician held his own. Instead of leading her like a pro and doing a plethora of showy moves, they danced together with a beautiful presence and calm connection as if they were alone and had all the time in the world instead of on a stage with an audience-packed house of people observing every move. But even as he led her, somehow, it seemed as if *she* was leading him and coaxing him to a special place. Clearly he knew how to dance tango almost as well as he knew how to play it on violin.

The *before* was the musician when he was in his domain and the *after* was the musician without his instrument. For a second he was a fish out of water but the minute he acquiesced and agreed to dance he made that transformation to be just a guy on the dance floor with a woman who chose him to dance with. And then in an instant, *he* was back in his domain albeit another sort of domain. Strong men, strong women, strong people: what is more romantic than equals meeting each other halfway? Given the applause they received afterwards clearly showed that the audience appreciated the moment as well.

Tango is always wooing you through romance only to show you that up close and personal it's really about people reaching out to other people for that singular moment where you speak the same language but wordlessly. You connect, you let go and you begin again.

CHAPTER ELEVEN

THE TANGO RAINBOW OR WHEN HE WAS A SHE WAS A THEM

Holly came from Miami, F.L.A.
Hitch-hiked her way across the U.S.A.
Plucked her eyebrows on the way
Shaved her legs and then he was a she

… She says, "Hey, babe
Take a walk on the wild side"
Said, "Hey, honey
Take a walk on the wild side"

Take a Walk on the Wild Side, Lou Reed

The world is evolving these days as never before insofar as social morays go. This is counter-pointed by the changing world of tango which always has its transitions which subtly unroll over time. Having been in tango for a long time and having returned to it post pandemic, I'm struck with the how things have morphed in the tango milieu. I've begun to appreciate how my perceptions are probably somewhat arcane. To be fair, my views on social morays, male/female dynamics in tradition settings and romance have always been old-fashioned. It's no secret to those that know me that I'm definitely hard-wired with an 1830's sensibility. I'm sharing this as a full disclosure way or caveat to frame the fact that my views of feminine, masculine, leaders, and followers are similarly sexist. It's entirely possible that how I see things is a blatantly old school construct which I still wear like a second skin.

Having said that, as gender roles morph and everything is up for examination and reassessment one is has to accept that nothing is black and white or even a little gray. We live in fluid times as far as sexuality goes and tango is the most fluid of fluid. The world is always slower to adopt new norms or accept the un-mainstream but tango offers a welcome mat. If there is some new haircut or clothing style you see as mainstream, trust me – it was brewing in tango about five years prior.

Tango is the first to know about such things and like most of the art and cultural world; it's the canary in the mine.

When I began tango, there seemed to be plenty of assertive men who asked demure, patiently waiting women to dance. Then the women, at least in my community, rose to egalitarianism and were less patient and started asking the men to dance. Then gay men asked gay and straight women to dance but didn't, save for another tango venue at the time called *Queer Tango*, dance with other gay men. Then many women, straight and otherwise, began learning how to lead and asked everyone to dance. Most everyone agrees that knowing both roles in tango makes you better at each. Many women or followers I've spoken to have said that learning to lead is freeing and negates them sitting passively, waiting to be asked to dance and broadens the partners one can have.

In the old days, there were nuanced tiers to all of this like a secret language we all knew but never spoke out loud. People jockeyed for their 'level' of dance depending on their preferences which was based on a diverse criterion. Now, post pandemic I've noticed my new classes are decidedly non-binary. Even committed straight couples traded lead and follow roles back and forth, experimenting with leading and following each other. Straight and gay women dance with each other or with straight and gay men and there's what seems to be a dwindling mainstream core of heterosexual couples on the dance floor. It's a rainbow out there. It's fun, freeing, diverse and open and despite this bit of writing, no one really thinks about it or comments.

Tango as the trope-y dance of seduction has in this journey also become a 'dance sport' so to speak and anything goes. The red rose, swooning woman and Latin lover are long gone and now when I enter attend some soirées (nod to Tango Fabrika) what greets me is reminiscent of the multi-faceted inter-Galaxia bar seen in *Star Wars* and the energy is fantastic.

When I started tango back when it was the stereo-type of heterosexual normative it was old school romance and a *he/she* affair which is why one couple always stood out to me. Now they wouldn't cause a ripple but in those days it was interesting to watch a quiet transformation occur in this pair.

When He was a She was a Them

There once was a couple that I knew and *nicknamed the-she-that-would-be-he-that-would-be-them.* I met them at somewhat conservative tango place of mostly English speaking dancers in a sleepy Montreal suburb. I went there mostly for classes but also for their informal Sunday afternoon milongas. It was an easy-going place as afternoon tango places tend to be. The social stakes were lower than most of the other venues but at the price of less people and dancing options but there's always a trade-off.

A couple used to come to this quiet tango place each and every Sunday afternoon. He appeared to be a late forty-something academic in looks: average build, oak-coloured hair, studious glasses always on, and a wardrobe of plaid shirts and lose jeans. He seemed to be of sturdy Scottish stock although he was so bilingual you couldn't tell if his mother tongue was English or French. His wife was a stalky vintage, a French peasant farm-girl issue: broad but not heavy, florid-faced with a bit of ruddiness to it almost like a Flemish painting. Overall she was a sturdy woman with a wholesome face framed in shiny brunette hair worn in a tight bun. She tended to wear multiple layers of shapeless clothing much like a collision of Eileen Fisher, Etsy and Les Misérables. Everything was a layer of linen and cottons in various murky shades of mushroom or dusky purple or a greys and mosses. Like her build, the strata of clothing were also thick but interesting in their ombre effect. They weren't particularly masculine clothes; they were more like non-binary or non-descript. To me they resembled what you'd wear if you were about to enter the abbey as a novice along with Maria Von Trapp. I call it rustic Boho.

The couple were matched in height and they seemed like a delightful and harmonious pair, clearly in love with each other and tango. They had newly discovered the dance and were addicted, practising incessantly for whenever I was there, they were there, like clockwork. Quick learners, they didn't stay beginners for long and I observed how seamless their dancing became. He grew to be a really capable leader and she was a smooth and sure-footed follower. Both of them however were extremely serious, dancing as if it was an obligation or moral mission. Eventually, the mister forwent the glasses as he got more confident as a leader and his L.L. Bean plaid shirts gave way to vintage small paisley as well as a bevy of Hawaiian prints.

Those first shirts debuted in shades of navy, khaki and grey but pretty soon they segued to fiery orange, canary yellows and hot pinks. The missus, aka his wife, also began to loosen up and ditched the traditional heeled-tango shoes for a modest, stout heeled Oxford lace-up shoe that was what women sometimes wore as a practise shoe. They're solid and a little masculine but very serviceable for hours of dancing. Her multi-tiered clothes morphed into an unchanging standard outfit of black tuxedo pants and a button up white shirt, sometimes with a black tie.

Each week, the man grew more uninhibited and flamboyant in his dancing overall and far less contained. His shirts would untuck, his hair, which he took to growing out longer, went askew and he took bigger chances in his dance lead and embellishments.

By contrast the wife seemed to grow more dominant or assertive and even though she was still the follower, it was almost as if she was back-leading. One day I noticed she was leading exclusively altogether and he was the default follower, both of them studiously learning the new roles. Sometimes they re-assumed their old roles but more often than not, she led, he followed, and eventually, once switched they stayed switched. There was no longer any warm-up of him leading or taking turns back and forth between them.

To me, watching this transition unroll over time was almost like they came in as a traditional husband and wife with leader and follower roles. Then they became gender neutral for a while and it was almost as though they each passed right through each other and out the other side of each other and into their inverse opposites. She became the 'he' and he became the 'her' and created their own gender-neutral world of 'them'. What is that line from Flannery O'Connor? *Everything that rises must converge or is it: eventually everything becomes its opposite?*

In that cross-over, they both became actually, the more authentic version of themselves which is to say, tango birthed their different energies that may have been brewing all the time. Maybe he was always a more passive, feminine man and she was meant to be the more assertive, directing energy. Separately and together, they represented a blurry part of a spectrum. Clearly, they found a way that worked for them.

Once the transition was complete, the only blip to it was if they came to tango alone any night. In those cases, the husband went back to being a traditional leader and his wife, if she was alone, returned to the follower role.

Nowadays, in contrast to that time years ago, no one wouldn't even notice such a couple. You have men learning to follow and women learning to lead in part because when you know both parts, you become a better dancer overall. Hetero couples switch back and forth in leading and following and gender is an afterthought tango insofar as the roles people perform. All the teachers have to know and demonstrate both the lead and follower role. I've

In all my years of tango, I don't feel I've learned nor perfected my follower's part as well as I aspire to and I'd rather be a responder and create from that role than the role of the initiator. I suppose that says something else about me but it's also because I am a good listener and observer. I like the conversation that unfolds in front of me and how my body, both with the listening aspect and whatever dance skills I have, 'talking' back in the role I prefer. I imagine how much disagreement other tango dancers might feel with my stance but if you can't be honest about this essential thing or are lying to seem 'woke' or trendy than that's far worse. It is simply what it is or how I am.

Interestingly other social dances the roles are called *leader* and *follower* or *follow* but in tango, perhaps because I learned tango in French-led classes, it's *guideur* (guider) and *guidee* (follower) which is a kinder, gentler way of describing the roles. To me, regardless of where on the rainbow spectrum you fall, I would describe it more as the 'speaker' and the 'listener'. Tango is a silent conversation but it's one of the most indelible ones I know. I like this inaudible conversation because as a writer I'm thinking *all the time* or talking or writing. So much of my day job is about *words* and at times I still never really hone on what I really want to say. But in tango, your body does all the talking and it's absolutely exquisite and at best, an equitable back and forth. There isn't a false phrase or wrong verb and there's a softly punctuated beginning and an ending to each dialogue of dance.

I've since seen that same couple I chatted about above and observed how they remained 'crossed over', happy and evidently still tango-ing only now as they did then but now the world has caught up to them and they blend right in or it's that everyone else blends in with them.

CHAPTER TWELVE

THE TANGO OR ALFAJORES COOKIE ADVENTURE

Early on in the days of my baking website, betterbaking.com, a Washington, D.C. reader asked me about something called **Alfajores Cookie.** I had never heard this cookie although it was described it sounded wonderful: almond cookie sandwiches with a caramel filling and sides rolled in coconut. This was before Google is the motherlode of information we now know and utilize every minute. In short, there was a time where there weren't a whole lot of places to research and it became a cookie odyssey.

One evening another dancer at one of my classes, a Chilean psychologist revealed the mystery. She explained these are very popular cookies are from Latin America but they're almost the national cookie of Argentina although they are also beloved in Bolivia, Chile, Colombia, Ecuador, Paraguay, Peru, the Philippines, Puerto Rico, Southern Brazil, Southern France, Spain, Uruguay, and Venezuela. Unfortunately my dancing friend didn't have a recipe to share but at least now I had a lead.

I found an *alfajores* cookie in one old cookbook on international desserts at the library but it didn't really describe the caramel filling. In fact it just said: *Fill cookies with caramel filling.* I went as far as to call the Argentinian, Chilean and Peruvian consulates in Montreal but (surprise) there was no help there. Finally found a Peruvian restaurant in the city and reached out. After fumbling with various permutations of English, French and Spanish, the baker, Ingala, who prepared them for the restaurant, informed me that she had no intention of parting with the recipe nor would she disclose any of the elements which I suppose, was fair enough. I told her I'd drop by and buy some of the cookies. She advised to call ahead as they sold out faster than she could bake them and would need to reserve them.

I arrived at the restaurant it was lunch time. Copious seafood plates, bowls of fresh soup, strange side dishes of spices and condiments, the scents of lime and scallion permeated the air. I snagged a take-out bowl of *Sopa de Casa,* a house soup of a chicken broth with scallions, lime and noodles to go with a clutch of the cookies. I wolfed down the hot soup since I could hardly wait to try the cookies. They were like shortbread but with ground almonds, a powdered sugar topping, a caramel filling that was like crème caramel or Quebec sugar pie and all topped with confectioners' sugar. But what *was* that distinct filling?

My Chilean tango friend enlightened me and told me it was *dulce de leche* – national treat of Latin America and not yet a trend or as ubiquitous (Costco sells it!) as it now is.

Back in the day, unless you'd travelled or are Latinx yourself you probably wouldn't be aware of what *dulce de leche* was. Since it wasn't easily available I had to make it myself. It's rather simple and it's only one ingredient: condensed milk. Using a double boiler, condensed milk is simmered for several hours until the milk becomes thickened and caramelized. Experienced *dulce de leche* makers simmer the entire sealed tin (minus the paper wrapper) in water but a warning on the tin recommends this procedure not be followed. I decided to heed the warning.

Many test batches and countless pounds of butter later; I think I may have broken the *Alfajores* code! These are superb cookies! They're elegant, unique and utterly delicious. They might not taste *exactly* like the commercial *Alphajores* you might have had in Buenos Aires or picked up in a Latin foods store but the coconut-edged almond cookie with its *dulce de leche* filling is most faithful to the essential part of *Alphajores*. It's a combination I never would have thought of and it's just one more thing I have to thank tango for. The only thing I did change in my own recipe is to use more flour *instead* of the hefty amount of cornstarch usually called for. I'm not a fan of cornstarch in baking but it does offer a lightness of texture. If you want that exact texture, swap half the flour in the recipe below for cornstarch. Although *dulce de leche* is available in supermarkets everywhere, nothing but nothing beats making your own. It just tastes so much better and there are no additives or anything else added. It's a pure and simple caramel made of simmered condensed milk. That's it. It's an ingredient also welcome in cheesecakes, ice-cream toppings, and squares.

Everyone calls these *Alfajores Cookies* but to me they will always be simply *Tango Cookies,* named after two of my passions: tango and baking. This recipe is in my second cookbook, *The Best of Betterbaking*.com as well as on my website_and now you have it here.

I hope you make some soon, enjoy a plateful and then make sure you keep dancing to keep off the calories.

Tango Cookies or Alfajores (Almond and Caramel cookies)

The dulce de leche filling should be prepared a few hours or a day ahead and refrigerated. These are incredible cookies of shortbread, caramel and coconut trim.

Dulce De Leche Filling

2 cans condensed milk

Cookie Dough

1 1/2 cups unsalted butter
1 cup confectioner's sugar
3 tablespoons granulated sugar
1 egg
2 tablespoons cream
1 teaspoon pure vanilla extract
1/4 teaspoon salt
1/4 teaspoon pure almond extract
1/3 cup ground almonds
3 cups all-purpose flour
Coconut

For the filling, spoon condensed milk into the top of a double boiler and set over simmering water. Stir occasionally, allowing milk to simmer for 3-6 hours on very low heat. Eventually, the milk will thicken and turn a deep caramel or deep butterscotch color. Cool well (it will thicken further) and refrigerate until needed.

For the cookie dough, in a mixer, cream the butter with the powdered sugar and granulated sugar until fluffy. Blend in the egg, vanilla and cream until well blended. The fold in the salt, vanilla and almond extracts, almonds and flour and mix to make a soft dough.

Wrap in plastic or place in a Zip Lock bag and refrigerate 30 minutes. (If you refrigerate for a few days or a few hours, you will have allow the dough warm up a bit before it can be rolled. Or, do what professional pastry chefs do: wack it with a rolling pin until it is a bit more in the mood to be rolled out). If it does not roll out easily, let it warm up a bit.

Roll out cookies on a lightly floured board to a thickness of 1/4 inch thick. Cut in 2 1/2 inch to 3 inch circles, preferably using a serrated or fluted edge cookie cutter. Bake on a parchment lined cookie sheet at 350 F. for 12-14 minutes. Cool well.

Spread some dulce de leche caramel filling on a cookie. Top with another cookie and press together nicely. Be careful, these are fragile. Spread some extra dulce de leche filling on the sides and roll in coconut. Dust the tops with confectioner's sugar

Makes about 25-35 cookies, depending on size

CHAPTER THIRTEEN

THE FOUR SEASONS OF TANGO: WINTER
WINTER SOLSTICE TANGO OR LAST TANGO OF THE YEAR

There's something extra special about pre-winter holiday tango, especially if you live in a frosty white and twinkly December city like Montreal. In summer, Montreal is a sexy coquette: a bit Paris, a bit New York but all the while she's still indelibly herself, warm-natured and lay-back. But by late November, she tucks in her skirts. In these parts, the December air here is dry, crystal and sharp and there's a taut anticipation to it. The sun glints rather than shines, casting a shimmery light against the darkness of the early sun-setting afternoons. Instead of the golden hour there is a frantic dusk-to-evening doh-see-doh as commuters scurry home from downtown seeking the coziness of the home front before the night really settles in. Personally, I've never liked that time of day especially in November and December unless I'm inside and already cozied away. There's just something about the 4 pm – 6 pm transition that's off-putting. But if you dance tango, you're in luck because you have a reprieve from the chill and one very much worth the risk of going out during this bleary part of day to seek a sunny haven.

All you have to do is find your way to a quiet, unassuming, drop-in tango studio on a cold, Sunday mid-afternoon when so many tango schools have practicas or informal *milongas.* These are relaxed times where you can drop by for a few dances or linger for the whole afternoon. Both practicas and milongas are usually filled with people from your regular tango classes and dancers from other schools or the occasional tourist, thirsty for their tango fix and an occasion that is easier going than classes or a soirée where the stakes are higher. You can come in a fancy or casual dress, sports jacket and tie or Nikes and your best jeans; anything goes except scrolling your cell phone.

Of course, I have my own favorite place, which is in Old Montreal and perched three flights up in an unassuming building, adjacent a toney French restaurant. You scoot up the stairs, tango-shoe bag in hand and heave the industrial door open. Tumbling inside from the hallway landing, you land in the planet's best kept secret, a magic kingdom of dance and music that chases the winter blues away in a heartbeat and a few bandoneon chords. There, hidden from the cold and darkness of December is a hot spot of warmth, music and humanity.

I always have a distinct impression when I first open that door, of flying bodies, being tossed hither and thither in mad tango freedom fest with everyone moving to the music. I think of speakeasies of decades past and wonder if they were like this demi-monde world as well. *This* is where the winter sunlight hides and where there's an undeniable life force, fueled by a plethora of happy people enjoying a few hours of connection. This beautiful, movable tableau is Montreal winter tango.

I remember one particular mid-December afternoon a few years ago. It was last practica before the New Year, before the crush and prioritizing of the holidays, other commitments and the multitude of other ways to celebrate the season with family and friends.

Winter Solstice Tango or Last Tango in the Year

Delicately navigating the highway and icy city streets, I arrived late and began to wonder what I was doing venturing out when I could have been home reading a good book or online gift shopping. But when I arrived, there was that pulsating before-holiday feeling in the air. So many people were there, both old friends and new ones in happy clusters around the dance floor. Immediately I was asked to dance and continued to have invitations, mostly from the men from my classes or fellows I've known for years but also a few newbies. Many or most tango people prefer familiarity and the ease of knowing friendly partners. I too appreciate that but nothing beats that unknown adventure dancing with someone you've never danced with before. It can be disaster or heaven and that's the risk and reward. The surprise of the afternoon was the last guy, about 24 or 25 years old, weighing ninety-nine pounds wet. He looked like he was at a frat party the night before and woke up in his clothes and running shoes and just rolled into tango. But surprisingly he was a treasure trove of style and he had an innate, flawless sense of rhythm. We did one *tanda,* each dance as smooth as silk. The *second* tanda began after a set of waltzes and then the music changed to *Nuevo* tango. My lead spoke his first and only words: *"Bon - contemporaire'* which I took that to mean: "*Oh now I have to switch gears and re-navigate -this is a whole new ball game, musically speaking*". For a minute I thought he would balk at the alternative tango music (some men have left me on the floor when the music changed to a milonga let alone Nuevo!) or would fumble in his lead but he was fantastic!

He was as good at the new music as he was with the waltzes. There's just something about *Nuevo* music and style tango with its rogue rules and unique form or obtuse angles that makes it double the magic carpet ride, especially with someone you don't know. All you need to go on this voyage is your basics of tango and a bit of trust. It's pretty simple: the leader makes space and invites you to take up that space. You listen and respond and move into that space. The result of this is the possibility to dance in a more choreographic way with more expressive creativity. One's inner dancer instincts get to experiment in a totally different, adventurous way that is often far more dramatic than traditional tango. That has much to do too with the fact that Nuevo tango music has different origins than traditional tango. You can dance it to *Sting* or *Billie Eilish* and it's still tango.

Soon enough, snow began falling outside. Many dancers had left and the bars of *La Cumparsita* the last tango, signaled the practica was over. I waved goodbye to friends, both those sitting and to some still dancing. I headed out into the chilly night, the streets gleaming with dainty, new snow, the sort that melts as it falls leaving black streets and white sidewalks. I slid into my car, reached for a pink patterned thermos I picked up in Chinatown the summer before. It was full to the frim with hot blackberry tea and honey I'd prepared beforehand. I sipped, started the car, turned on the calm of Chopin and began my way home. When I floated into my house, I was still in a tango cloud, despite being greeted with a house strewn for sofa-pillow forts, empty pizza and juice boxes and a relieved babysitter.

One/we/us/people all have to get out and find what makes us happy. Sometimes it takes at least a few tangos to get revved up but the joy I had that winter tango afternoon was enough to fuel me through evening and through the next morning in my day job as a cookbook author and carpooling mother of three sons.

Not too long from now I know the snow will visit, falling heavy and thick; instead of melting as the first snows do, this one will stay on the ground as winter comes to roost and burrow. When no one is looking, I'll be tangoing in the white-sheeted park near my house, the little park hidden among the trees. If you happen to take a walk and find a pattern of circular footsteps in the snow and hear the faint sounds of a phantom bandoneon playing *Adios Nino,* you'll probably figure out I've been there earlier, doing my own private winter tango.

CHAPTER FOURTEEN

ON THE SUBJECT OF MEN WHO DON'T DANCE TANGO

Overheard: two women talking, in the hallway, outside the dance hall of a tango studio.

Hola – Long time, no see! You haven't been here in a while.

Yes - I met someone!

Is it serious?

I think so. It's been a few months. It's going well.

Does he tango?
(Cautiously) No.

Is he interested in learning?

He says he might try it.

(Sympathetically) I understand. I really hope it works out.

(Slightly despondent) Me too. He's really special but I can't give up tango.

Well, of course not. Who could?

Of course, the man that you're dating, especially if it's a new relationship, is likely to be somewhat disinterested in your tango life unless he was considering tango himself and/or you've invited him and he said yes or he was trying to be polite date one through three. Tango folks learn to accept that few people are as interested in our dance passion as we are. Some romantic partners don't care one way or another but it depends where you are in the relationship and the contender in question. Tango is not like any other pursuit. You can try explaining until the cows come home that it's 'tango is only dancing' and not necessarily romantic but it's not easy.

Let's be frank, tango is not chess or fly fishing – there's another sort of man/woman dynamic that's always present when you mix people up and have them dance with each other, chest to chest and cheek to cheek.

But to even consider giving up tango in service to having a relationship outside tango, and more than a few people do this at various times, is like paring off a piece of your soul to make it fit shoes that were a barely-fit to begin with.

"It's just weird" commented a guy I once dated, '*to dance with a total stranger, someone you don't even know their name and in such proximity. It's not…natural'*.

But what that guy and outsiders to tango don't grasp is that the tango addiction is *all* about that unnatural/natural act of fusing to a stranger for a few dances. It can be sensual or comforting and it's (often) awkward, (frequently) lyrical, an epic fail or the biggest (and shortest) romance of your life. But each time, you have this chance to go on a huge adventure with another conspirator. It can be a fiasco or a bore or it can be so utterly transportive that I still pinch myself when that happens.

It's no secret that tango is neither for those who don't like to be touched nor for those that wince at the proximity of strangers. Tango is for those that have hungry souls that are slaked temporarily by other hungry souls who are craving this connection even if it only happens rarely and always totally unexpectedly.

One woman I once spoke with, a tall, blond math student confessed, *"I have to sneak out to tango. I tell my boyfriend I'm having a drink with my girlfriends. He doesn't dance and has zero interest in learning. He simply can't see why I must and so I lie. I left him home hours ago, fast asleep on the couch watching some reality show. Before I return, I will change my shoes and splash water on my face and neck (to wash off the scent of any aftershave). This way, he doesn't ask and so far, and it's been months, he seems to not notice anything. I hate lying but I can't give up tango'.*

I used to tell people outside the dance circle that *you don't meet anyone at tango* because too often I've seen the same men and women line the tango floor, sipping their solitary glass of wine and dancing with who they know or occasionally a new person but I don't always see much romance happening. Then there are those who fall in love with their default partners, drop them and move on or alternatively marry them and always come to tango with them.

Chances are more likely romance occurs *outside* tango. You take on new person in your life and at the beginning and middle you drop out of tango. New romances might not support you going off on a Friday or Saturday night to tango so what happens is that one drops tango. Alas, it's collateral damage of the new relationship. First you hold onto the class tango but then I've seen so often, even that goes by the wayside. The up side however about romances that *don't* work out is that there is still and always tango and someone to catch you. But if you lose tango? Well, that outside thing better figure in the soul mate column because that is a major sacrifice.

But what would it be like to either find someone at tango? How would it be to be held by a man you were attracted to in mind, body, spirit and dance with *him*? How would it be to dance with someone you could see caring for or be with outside in the real world? Could there be a union that retains its magic in and outside of tango? Must one always choose between one and the other? Do you have to choose between a soulmate and soulful tango? I think the *Holy Grail* of it all is that fusion. Does it exist? I don't know yet but I guess one day I might find out.

INTERLUDE

THE MAN WHO FELL IN LOVE TOO OFTEN

Last night at tango we danced in solidarity for the planet. Throughout the globe, tango places were open concurrently in their various time zones. There was live streaming of music from Buenos Aires, Paris, Los Angeles, and Montreal, to name just a few participating tango cities. It was a fund-raiser to combat global warming and it made for a unique and lovely evening of tango and humanity. It was a sea of old faces and new ones, swish of dresses, matching the music of various tango DJ's who contributed to the cause. There I met up with Daniel, a long time tango partner and incurable romantic. Daniel is a tango friend who always worries the women he dates that he's met at tango will dance with other men and be spirited away once they change partners. What he fears is that after a few dances with another man she'll leave Daniel and take up with someone new – fast and unequivocally.

"But Daniel, I said, "*Tango people know better than that. We don't fall in love with each person we dance with!"*

"You really believe that so? Don't you think we're all strange, dancing with other people, held close, and moving intimately? Is this not a recipe for disaster?"

"*No. I assure you, women are not that susceptible to a good lead. We know who is a good dancer and who we love....if and when we do fall in love with someone at tango or anywhere else.*"

Daniel has been desperately searching for love on the dance floor ever since I first met him, once wide-eyed, hopeful and romantic. Now, a few years later, not unlike a few tango men and women, he's slightly disenchanted, moving from embrace to embrace, dance to dance, never finding only thirsting and searching anew each time a dance is done. Which dance is that you ask? Good question. Of course it's that infernal, eternal one about love in that '*are we there yet*' theme.

As we danced, I listened to him talk and came to appreciate it was really about *him* not finding the one woman, with whom he is a true fit in all ways - and a woman who will see him for who he is and stay with him, beyond the dance. He just hasn't gotten there yet and so he has transferred the doubts he has to tango. Because if it *is* about how *tango* corrupts love and challenges loyalty, then it's not a story about him. Instead, it becomes about how women are fickle, flit and finally flee. So I listened to him talk and like all of us, we create theories from very personal moments hoping to see a pattern and escape the sense that maybe it *is* about us and then we have to deal.

Many tangos later, I know who is a good leader and who I am drawn to as a man. One learns what is real and what has off the dance floor potential and what doesn't; where the substance and resonance is, in tango and without.

Tango *is* strange and few disagree with that. You're in a stranger's embrace every new tanda. And sure, there's some promiscuity as there is in any social situation, there's a loyalty of the heart and spirit and it supersedes all else, even the steamiest close embrace. The best leader in the world, i.e. *Pablo Veron*-magical can't really take your heart off course. But to know this, you have to have fallen in love at least once in your life. And once you do, you return to tango changed from the inside out. It's the anti-venom for tango's inky tentacles. Otherwise maybe you would indeed disappear with each new partner on the merit of better fine footwork and a better after-shave thinking each one is *the one* or *a one*.

My friend Daniel has never been in love and all the women he holds he only holds briefly. They are rentals. No wonder why he worries and why each new dance and each new person is part of a quest. He's a pretty good tango dancer but what he doesn't know about love, to quote a line from *Moonstruck*, is a lot.

TANGO WITH THE ONE

Last night I had the
Dance of my life
With a man I did not know
He held out his hand
And drew me on the floor
I heard the music start
And the stars stuck a chord
I felt the touch of his hand
And his breath on my cheek
The beat of his heart
Was stayed by heat,
Within two bars
I knew his every motion
Matched my steps
To suit his devotion
I floated on a cloud
We never had to speak
But -

He wasn't you
And it wasn't the same
No matter how he led
No matter how in synch
I could waltz with him
Glide in perfect harmony
A million eternities
And still -
He wasn't you.
And I knew it in each beat

If ever I am in your arms again
I will dance on the spot
If ever I touch you again
I'll move to the music
I know by heart
Let my spirit dance free
While my soul takes off.
Because he wasn't you.

CHAPTER FIFTEEN

THE SOULMATE LIST: MUST LOVE TANGO OR BE WILLING TO LEARN

I finally added *Must Love Tango* or *Be Willing to Learn* on my soulmate list. I can no longer pretend that it doesn't matter or it's a casual add-on as in likes nature and long walks. It's too important.

When I first began tango there was unspoken intention most of us have of meeting someone *at* tango and then experience that connection off and on the dance floor, happily twirling away into the sunset? But what all of us find about tango is that in the beginning it's a challenge to just stay upright, lead or follow with a modicum of grace, not sweat until you're dripping and above all, not fall flat on your face. But then something else happens. You stop caring about meeting *him or* her because *each* tango, *each* tango venue, *each* tango evening offers unlimited possibilities of perfect tango strangers with whom to trip the light fantastic. You become entirely different people with all and each of them and that's riveting stuff. However fleeting the dances, and each one overlaid with other partners and dancers, it's about an addictive connection that stays with you.

But then one day you realize that you've danced with a multitude of men. By my own count I've done the math: over two decades of tango, at least one lesson a week, one practise evening and one soirée. Each tango outing is an opportunity to dance with at least six or more partners. Add to this the people you dance with at the partner switch in classes. So that's eighteen partners times let's say, forty-eight weeks or so in any particular year (counting in weeks here or there I've missed tango) and that's over five thousand men, discounting teachers who have whirled me around to demo steps or turns. Just to be clear: that is over 5000 men. Sometimes I dance with someone and I don't remember their face or name but as soon as they hold me I remember: *ah yes, that one. I recall this embrace.*

There have been exceptional dances and terrible ones and mostly the dances have fallen into the category of: pleasant/lovely/fine.

This also happens when you no longer pout after a bad night of tango or care unduly if you dance less than you might have wanted to. You no longer imagine the equation of: a great dance = a great guy= a possible relationship.

You become more discerning. Coincidentally, this all happens when your skill level is at its peak which is to say, you're hungry but not starving because part of your soul's hunger is fulfilled by superb dancing and great connections. And *that's* the precise moment you realize: you want someone special and preferably someone who also dances tango or be willing to learn. It's hard to compartmentalize such core things in your life and the experience of dancing with your significant other is undeniably unique.

Tango is the original 'dance' in courtship terms, that one step forward, one step back deal. There's a certain resolution in the embrace, denunciation, articulation, chase, pause, capture and then it all repeats. It's all there on the dance floor –unfolding, never ending, mini seductions that lives in syncopated, quarter notes. Off the dance floor, the dance is called *The Game. The game* is what you do when you are not sure of where you want to be and whom you want to be with and the game lets you buy time while you prevaricate. Conversely, *the dance* is what you do when you are pretty sure you want to be there but you are playing with the pacing so that you can savor every beat, every touch and every motion that is an emotion away.

So if you see someone who seems like he could be my guy please let him know this: he must know how to tango or be willing to learn. Because I can learn to put the cap on the toothpaste and be careful about not throwing out Styrofoam out with the recycling and while it makes me cringe, I can tolerate teabags versus tea-leaf tea but please, please, *please,* (unmet guy) be willing to come with me to tango, hold me in your arms and lead me in the softest, kindest, slowest possible cover of Astor Pizzazollo's *Oblivion.*

Ok – let's back up. *Maybe* this isn't really the case 100%. Soulmates and tango partners can be mutually exclusive and that's just as fine. Instead, I think the man in my life should just encourage me to go out and enjoy myself dancing, knowing I will return. I don't need him to also dance tango. He just has to be present in the other million ways that count and might count more. And he has to be able to say this and really mean it: *have a good time at tango tonight!*

CHAPTER SIXTEEN

THE TANGO WARS

These days there's something different about tango. I hate to admit it but like an irritating pea under the mattress, something is just 'there' and whatever *it* is, it's ruining things. The truth is that tango has been different for the longest time and I've tried both ignoring and pretending it's fine but like that damned pea under the mattress - you *feel* it. You turn this way and that and you still feel it and you have to deal.

For one thing, too often in the last while, I go to tango and I sit. And wait. And sit. I don't even really mind because I look across the dance floor and assess the men and realize that I don't even like dancing with this one or that one. This one leads too fast, that one leads too quick; this one insulted my style once, and another one was a critical partner in a tango class and I swore I wouldn't ever dance with him if he was the last man on the planet (or at tango). But it's really not fun to sit indefinitely.

At home, before tango, I do my dance-centric toilette and arrive each time, fresh, perfumed, hair just so and beautifully dressed.

My shoes are aching to dance; *I* am aching to dance. And once there time stands still. The music mocks me because I who feels like (we all do!) the very essence of tango is planted there like a stuck-in-mud wallflower.

But something else, aside from my own *ennui* is happening and has been happening for a few years now. Men come to tango already with partners in tow or only ask the same one or two women to dance. They don't ever change partners! The same people come to every milonga like a roving group of the usual suspects. You begin to feel there's no fresh air. The music is the same and that's hardship enough. How you can tap into new feelings and alternate steps and experiment if they play the same *Di Sarli melody* over and over? Of course, a good dancer and someone who isn't feeling a tad sour can indeed tap into new things but that's another discussion. But mostly it's like the soul of tango seems gone. Like gum that's lost both its taste and its sweetness and all that's left is that redundant rubbery chewiness. At the least, I notice people are not adventuresome in their steps. They've also stopped dressing up. They come in jeans and running shoes. People don't seem to want to improve.

They dance by rote – like robots. There's no mystery but there are politics. A creepy, subtle culture that is a weird impassivity or slightly hostile passivity has taken place. There's no smoke, no fire, and no spirit. Some people have begun the habit of scrolling on their cell phones while dancing! Am I the only one who notices? Is this an inside thing or outside thing?

On *Facebook*, yes oh my goodness, there's tango on *Facebook* and *Instagram, Reddit* and *Tiktok* now! When I began tango, the Internet was one year old! Now it's new tango of the digital era. And this is another thing; once tango was a place where cell phones were banned. Now everyone videos every dance and before you can say *Hola, would you like to dance* the bit of video is on YouTube. Like everyone else, in this day and age, no one is present, just *watching* or *dancing* tango in real time. They're recording it and uploading it and sending out links. Every upload, every tango cross chat on Facebook and the feeling of tango, the realness of it at least for me, leaches out just a little more. I resent that *nothing* seems sacred and that the tango 'Walden Pond' is now like NYC's Central Park during Fleet Week.

Sometimes people even get into disputes on Facebook as tango discussions become heated. Not passionate 'heated' – but hostile in cyber chat room edginess. *What is 'real' tango – what is no longer officially tango? What is better, Nuevo or classical tango music? Which schools have bad teachers or bad vibes*? Sometimes the Facebook discussions just seem like another version of Republicans versus Democrats or any other boring, long-standing oppositional factions. In analyzing tango so much they are desecrating its essence, interrupting the 'it' factor of tango by verbalizing *everything* about something which you can only paw at describing. You have to explore it; you have to dance it. They're taking this adventure to a mystical land and attaching it to a Disney map that keeps proclaiming: *You Are Here.* I don't want to be told where I am. I want to discover it myself! There are so few real adventures left anymore.

I dislike *all* of it. I dislike how the romance and mystery seems gone. It's certainly not the same subtly of the tango that first greeted me ages ago. Today's tango seems at times no different than a busload of people seeking any distraction got dropped off and splat into tango. Plus if you dare confide to anyone else that tango has changed, you're judged for 'living in the past and loving nostalgia".

Yes, I love nostalgia if it means a time when people were nicer, men were more gallant, even nicely marginal, a little raw and I actually danced (instead of sitting) when I went to tango.

At first I just wouldn't accept that tango had changed. I went at different times and days and to different venues. But the well continued to dry out. I felt myself segue from being the *Tango Empress* and I became the *Tango Crone* – angry, bitter and sitting on the sidelines, analyzing everyone on the dance floor. I complained to friends and other tango dancers. I tried ballroom, I went to *Lindy Hop* and *West Coast Swing* class, *Semba* and *Contra Dancing* which was a minor but significant error in judgment. No one told me how group-oriented *Contra* was. Fun, yes. Romantic? No. The itch remained and I missed tango the way you miss a boyfriend who doesn't even know or care that you've left. I began to think tango was divorcing me or forcing me to leave. So I started to stay away in service to denying that something had altered. I've never been good at falling out of love with things I love nor given things time and space to rest. I'm like that horse that runs back into the burning barn.

And then one day in that same period of time, I went to an industrial park to investigate a wholesale bath and tub store. Across from the bath-tub store I noticed a sign that said: ***Why Not Dance?*** A dance school! I called the number on my phone from the car and left a message. Minutes later I got a text saying there was a free tango class the following week that I could attend. I texted back: *yes – I will be there.* It was free; it was nearby; what was the risk?

When I arrived I found but three couples (well, a young man was without a partner and together, we made up the third couple) and a solitary teacher (not a couple). Pretty soon, given this was a beginner class, it was evident I was a ringer. The teacher used me as the demo dancer. The men (all three) who had to take turns dancing with all the women noted how I was a pleasure to dance with and had I danced before?

Afterwards the teacher and studio owner came to talk to me and asked who I really was. Turns out the teacher knew all the people and tango places I did. In heavily Spanish accented English she said: *I've been to Buenos Aires – all over – the world over – and tango has changed! It has lost its soul'.* Her eyes gleamed and her face reflected profound love and she seemed a bit bittersweet and I could connect to that.

I agreed but told her, "*Dancing in this beginner class, where everyone was not yet jaded or part of the new and chillier tango culture, I had a great time.*" She said she was happy to hear it. The fact was, I could feel my blood starting to thaw and I wanted to come back the following week and perhaps take the technique class.

The teacher then asked my last name and said: *But you're Jewish! I am too – but Argentinean Jewish* (her grandparents, as mine did, fled Russia in 1920). She hugged me and I left after that, feeling the cold of the winter air cool down my flushed cheeks and warm face.

The class had been quite a work out and exciting – like a homecoming. Back at the beginning, in a dance school in an industrial park with total newbies I found a nugget of tango soul. No one filmed the class with their smart-less phone, everyone was discovering the dance for the first time and the joy of it, laughing as they fumbled steps and bumped noses. It's wasn't sexy or sultry but it was unfettered, real and fun. There were no stakes and it was light-hearted.

At any given time, there's a tango war ongoing. It can be inside you or outside – a mood or a pandemic. When it's the latter, there's even some comfort in knowing that because if so many of us feel it and miss the old tango (the second Golden Age of tango) then the soul has to still be there but hiding. Like all things, it will morph, or rest and then re-emerge. It will be better perhaps but for sure, it will be different. But between the what-was-ness of the tango I was mourning and the tango that had-not-yet-arrived, I had found a cease-fire and in so doing, quenched my thirst and made peace. Sometimes you just need a pause and then you can return to what you love.

The Sabbatical and the Tonic

One day a hard-to-identify season of tango sprouts up out of the blue. It inevitably comes *just as* you were starting to relax and really fall in love with tango and about to propose marriage or otherwise commit forever. It comes at a saturation point where your dance skills climb as high as never before and so it's ironic that just as all was well and good in sweeps this chilly breeze. It's such a paradox and I think it has to do with refusing to take a sabbatical from even your favorite passions. Even true love needs a respite to collect and repair but how we balk!

This malaise is evidenced by a slight fatigue that you try and outrun and you do your best to not think about it. If you don't name it, you tell yourself, perhaps it will just go away. It's burn-out at the behest of a drought of spirit. Reluctantly, you notice as you attend your usual venues that, class by class, milonga by milonga, that you're just not getting the tango you want and need. Even bad tango, like relatively good tango but the better you get, the more demanding you are and hard to satisfy and the more it all feels like going through the motions. There's an itch you can't reach. So you double down on the drug that usually works but it just feels like you're a hack horse at a petting zoo and you think of simply going home and reading a good book. No matter what you do, no matter who you dance with, no matter where you go and what music is played, the magic, as they say, is gone. So many of us get to that point at some point but the first time it strikes is the longest and most alarming.

At first, you don't understand and you throw yourself at tango determined to recapture what you used to have but like all burn out it's like a fire that turns in on itself and loses its fuel for it is eating its very source. I guess the first time I experienced it, there were a few provocations but it was like I could only see tango through a negative filter which is how you see everything when you're burnt out.

Increasingly, I saw people partner up for classes. Instead of showing up and dancing with someone new or that you know but didn't dance with before, I saw couples all come to class and I was one of the few people person who came alone.

At first, I didn't catch on until the tango workshop when *even there,* despite the fact more than half the class was from out of town, and you would think that the tango stray cats would dominate. But e*ven* there, *even* then, everyone came arrived in pre-set tango partnerships forged quietly off the dance floor in stealthy text notes or emails or drinks shared after class. Somehow I've never been part of those secret handshakes in and out of tango. I've always been a solo practitioner.

But between everyone competing for partners (and deliberately, not switching to someone beside them in the partner switch) I began to see a new tango culture evolving or maybe one that was always there that I was oblivious to. Whereas I was willing to take a chance and come to tango solo and expand my horizons a new tango mainstream had formed – one that was as (relatively) safe as Arthur Murray dance studios. I felt isolated when I concluded that *even* at tango, I was the odd one out.

It took many evenings of going home disgruntled or once in tears, until I came to accept we are all different. If I'm unique in being willing to take a chance and find another great partner (or terrible one or no one) then stay with the tried-and-true-settling poor partner in order to be comfortable, then so be it. But what that implied about the renegade world of tango I thought was its core was an implication I was not ready to face. Or conversely, what it said about me even at tango was the same lesson I already have learned about me and life which is still: sure, we're all unique but some of us are more unique. As a consequence, it's a theme that plays out no matter where you show up. I did a lot of soul searching about this until I accepted that a) I might have concluded wrongly and had a moody bias that colored my view or b) I best develop a both harder shell and a strategy because I certainly wasn't ready to quit tango.

So, with no small feeling of reluctance, I took a break from tango. I needed to regroup, recharge and organize my thoughts and feelings and fill my life with some new things so I can appreciate tango again. I've learned to do this each and every time that burn-out shows up. I go to that sabbatical place. I take the time to shop for perfumes, candles and incense or listen to new music while on a park walk, read new books, visit art museums and vintage stores and generally haunt the city streets on urban adventures. I hunt for new coffees and bubble tea, wander and people watch.

It's so difficult to let go of the world I adore so much and relax, knowing, that if I but let it go, both it and me will re-unite in time. It's the most restorative part of my wellness life. When I do return to tango, I'll be somewhat rusty but my legs and feet will remember to follow and my heart will start beating in tandem with the tango music playlist without a hitch of a lost beat.

Sometimes you have to allow your spirit to mingle with other pursuits and then if it *was* true love, that thing you left, you'll begin to long for it again so much so that even an average dance with an imperfect stranger is all you need to jumpstart it again. A man will ask me to dance and in a bar or two we are off. I remember everything and yet I worried about forgetting! My legs become cat legs, lithe and sure and infused with muscle memory. I wonder, before I disappear in the current, how could I have left this for so long? And then the sheer bliss and joy of tango comes roaring back in one fell swoop. I swim, I float, I fly.

CHAPTER SEVENTEEN

BALLROOM DANCE OR A TANGO DANCER, LIVE AT THE COPA

Every once something in me gets a bit restless. When I do, I take a peek into the showcase window of ballroom dance, beguiled by this different world filled with sequins, rules, lyrical poses and old school elegance and glamour. Here's there's a ballroom dance place of some sort in almost every quarter of the city. I've also seen all the movies: *It's Strictly Ballroom, Shall We Dance* and *Marilyn Hotchkiss' Ballroom Dancing and Charm School.* I've watched enough *PBS* ballroom competitions back I the day to know something about ballroom. Oh, those flowing dresses, those arched backs! Without telling anyone where I am off to or why I am doing, I sneak off quell my restlessness and to indulge my summer past-time which is finding yet another free trial ballroom class.

Most places offer the 30-minute free lesson before they lock you in a room and try and get you to sign up for years and thousands of dollars of dance lessons. My local *Arthur Murray* studio is notorious for this but I discovered a promising place between uptown and downtown a while ago that I had to try. Seeing the huge sign blinking on and off in a second floor vintage building saying *Dance Studio*, *Waltz, and Cha-Cha* seemed to be my cue. It was nicely cheesy which always does the trick and I made registered for a trial appointment for the very next Saturday morning.

In the tiny studio's administrative office cubed off from the dance rooms I filled out the copious forms. They were overwhelming being just a little less long and complicated than the ones at a new dentist. Based on what I wrote in the spaces, the ballroom studio director determined I was a *beginner* (blithely ignoring my 10 years of tango and 25 years of modern, jazz and ballet). Fairly enough, in the world of ballroom, I was a babe in the woods. Officially, since they have competitive levels I was placed in *Bronze Level.*

"How competitive do you want to go?" asked the instructor.
I didn't know.
"How many hours of week are you willing to sacrifice to rehearse?"
I had no idea.

I got the sense that the ballroom dance was a little like signing a dance contract with the mob. Once in, you're a lifer. Either the passion for the dance, the zeal of the studio manager or copious forms would commit you for an eternity.

Finally, after all the forms were filled out, I was allowed on the dance floor where I received some minimalist instructions for a smattering of rumba, some waltz and cha-cha. They were all fun but the waltz was wonderful! I felt like a swan or a character that should be on a Disney princess float. Then with about seven minutes of the free trial remaining the teacher decided to teach me ballroom or continental-style tango.

"*You probably won't be able to follow my lead but just try and keep up*" said the teacher. I felt my tango engine purr like a *Ferrari.* I smiled and said I'd do my best and asked him to go slow.

For those seven minutes it was heaven. I wasn't sure if the teacher figured out I knew what I was doing but our lesson abruptly ended. Once again, I was cornered in that small office and pressed to commit to ballroom dance classes for a decade ahead to the tune of about ten years' of mortgage payments. Somehow I escaped with my Visa card unused and mumbled something about '*of course I'll come back when I decide'* and then fled down the stairs.

Of course, that wasn't and won't be the last free ballroom trial I sign up for. I'm addicted to those 30-minute trials. It keeps me on my toes to dance other dances, to learn how to listen to other sort of leads and it re-commits me to tango. That being said, I'm on the verge of running out of places that offer the 30-minute free trials or else word on the street is beginning to circulate that I'm a repeat offender. I'll have to just stop or (and perish the thought) agree to the multiple levels of *Bronze, Silver, and Gold.* If I do immigrate to ballroom on a fulltime basis I might never look back and tango might end up missing one tanguera. I have to admit, the costumes in the ballroom dance store that is beside their office are so beautiful. I love glitz! Perhaps a holiday from all-dressed-in-black might be in my future.

Ballroom Lessons
Where Cool Russian Meets Hot Latin

As it turned out I did commit for a few weeks; today was my Monday ballroom lesson which was adequate. There's always a new instructor but today's person was late. He was a tall, slick European fellow called Anatol sporting a copious dose of Aqua di Gio. He was so tall that my main focus was in avoiding this belt buckle which coincided with my nose. Suffice to say there was a physical inequity and I cursed that I didn't wear higher shoes.

To be frank, I found Anatol very patronizing or perhaps it just was in terms of style; tango guys and ballroom guys are quite different. I can't pinpoint it but if I had to compare I'd say tango men are somewhat edgy or marginal and Anatol was slick and showy. There was one other couple dancing with a female teacher instructing them while Anatol and I carefully winnowed in and around them. At one point they waltzed just as I was doing waltz and it seemed to me that the four of us were at a *My Fair Lady* rehearsal. But then the music segued to a brisk and dramatic tango. Now it's my turn I thought!

In contrast to Argentine tango, (to me) ballroom tango is almost comic and seems like a caricature of tango. It has none of the slink of Argentinean tango and the foot position is different. You lead with heel in ballroom whereas in Argentine tango, you never see the underside of your shoe. In ballroom, you throw this demure, aloof stare over the right shoulder of the male lead which seems like erstwhile femme fatale and such a pose. Overall, Argentine Tango is low-key and smooth whereas ballroom tango is quite herky-jerky. I tend to feel that while it's stunning, ballroom is form over content whereas Argentine tango is content over form. To put it more succinctly, ballroom is lifestyle set to music; tango is life. In ballroom tango, you're performing or posing. It's dramatic and exciting in its way but in Argentine tango, in my view, you're connecting on a deeper level. At the least, you're not performing; you're having a conversation with another person just for the two of you not for spectators.

Part of my displeasure was because Anatol, who seems to be a poseur in every respect, striking actual poses and checking his clothes and tan every time we drew close to the mirrors and telling me about wealthy clients he had. But the worse thing I can say about him and this is true of all bad leaders, no matter what genre of dance it is, is that he didn't *listen* and that to me is in dance, as it is in life, a non-negotiable.

I've discovered quite a few ballroom dance refugees in my tango classes and I can understand it. The reverse is less true. People don't leave tango to go and settle happily-ever-after at ballroom.

They might add *Salsa* or *West Coast Swing* to their tango but they don't double-down on *ballroom.* However, I do love the grace of ballroom and just look for the exit when it comes to those competitive levels as a participant.

Next week is my last ballroom class for this summer. I saw a pair of gold sequin dance shoes at a vintage shop with a 3 inch *Copa* heels which might work nicely for *Continental Fever Night.* I know, I know. How could I? What can I say? Who doesn't like dressing up? I'll be back at tango once the amateur competition and subsequent potluck dinner that follows it, all to be held next week is over and done.

I've included my favorite tango cake btw that works for any dance gathering or community pot luck.

Last Tango Cake

Whenever there's a tango pot luck or for tango festivals, I make this cake or try to. It's massive and feeds a crowd but mostly it's easy (ok, there's a few steps), moist, decadent and totally delicious. Garnish with a red rose to complete the 'tango' look. I created this cake to be sophisticated but crowd-pleasing and there's no great satisfaction for me than dancing and over the shoulder of my lead, noticing other dancers slicing into that cake! No but a few people know who made it and I like being anonymous. Most people at tango know I bake professionally but I keep it on the down low mostly so I can blend in and sail on the dance floor in my tango identity – not my baker one! This is a great cake to bring to a ballroom dance potluck too! You can also find this cake at my site, www.betterbaking.com.

Cake

2 cups sugar

1 ¼ cups unsalted butter, melted

4 eggs

2 teaspoons pure vanilla extract

2 3/4 cups all-purpose flour

1/2 teaspoon salt

1 1/2 teaspoons baking soda

1 1/2 teaspoons baking powder

1 cup cocoa, measured then sifted

1 1/2 cups warm coffee or cola

Simple Syrup

1/2 cup sugar

½ cup water

1 teaspoon chocolate extract, optional *

½ teaspoon pure vanilla extract

Whipped Cream Filling

1 ¼ cups whipping cream

1 teaspoon pure vanilla extract

2 tablespoons confectioners' sugar

Nutella Raspberry Dulce Filling

1 cup dulce de leche

1 cup Nutella, or hazelnut spread, softened

1/2 cup raspberry preserves

1 cup fresh raspberries

Chocolate Buttercream

1 cup unsalted butter, softened

3/4 cup cocoa

4-6 cups confectioner's sugar

2 teaspoons pure vanilla extract

¼-1/2 cup light cream

Ganache Glaze

1 cup whipping cream

1 ¼ cup chopped, semi-sweet (preferably Swiss) chocolate

Garnish
Red Rose
White chocolate, melted
Raspberries
Red sugar, for dusting

Preheat oven to 350 F. Lightly grease 2 9-inch layer pans and line with parchment paper circles.

In a large mixing bowl, blend sugar and butter. Add eggs, vanilla and mix until thick. In a separate bowl, stir together flour, salt, baking soda, baking powder, and cocoa. Fold dry ingredients into wet and mix, drizzling in coffee or cola as mixture blends. If using an electric mixer, use slow speed for about 3 minutes, scraping sides and bottom once to incorporate all ingredients evenly. This is a thin batter.

Bake, on middle rack, 40-50 minutes, until cakes spring back when lightly touched.

For the Chocolate Buttercream, cream the butter and vanilla with cocoa and 1 cup of the confectioner's sugar. Add remaining confectioner's sugar and whip on high speed, adding in cream to achieve a light, fluffy consistency. If not using right away, refrigerate but re-whip before using. Add additional warm water to get correct consistency (a tablespoon at a time).

For simple syrup, boil water and sugar 5 minutes and remove from heat. Stir in extracts.

For the whipped cream, whip cream with vanilla and confectioners' sugar until soft but firm peaks form.

For the Ganache Glaze, heat cream to just scalding and add in the chocolate. Remove from heat and whisk to blend/melt chocolate to make a thick glaze. Set aside (Refrigerate if not using right away and warm up slightly when needed).

Semi freeze the cake before decorating.

To decorate, slice each cake layer in two layers, using cardboard circles to remove two layers and set aside.

Serves 14-20

Place one layer on a cake stand that turns. Brush it with Simple Syrup and then spread on half the raspberry jam, and then the Nutella, and then the whipped cream. Dot on some raspberries on the whipped cream. Top with the second layer of cake, drizzle with syrup and then spread on the dulce de leche, and over that, about 1/2 inch of frosting. Repeat filling and layering with remaining two layers. Once cake is assembled, ice cake - sides first.

Ice cake all over with a thin layer of chocolate buttercream. Freeze 30 minutes and then pour Ganache Glaze over cake. Let set a bit. Then make a border on the bottom and top with more chocolate butter cream. Garnish with touches of melted white chocolate, fresh raspberries, and a dusting of red crystal sugar (like sugar for holiday cookies).

Refrigerate until serving. Serves 12-20

CHAPTER EIGHTEEN

CAFÉ LIMA, TIME FOR A LITTLE OLD SCHOOL TANGO

The other night I found a new tango place. According to *Facebook*, it had been open three years and had held many events but my dance card was full of the usual places and I was comfortable with the familiar. But one night, the stars converged and I knew it was time to try the new place which somehow had an old school sound to it.

As I drove to yet another part of town that I didn't know, I had my doubts and I cursed myself for not checking with Google maps beforehand. Similarly I cursed myself for not filling three-quarter empty car before setting off. As my stomach growled, I also realized I'd forgotten to eat and was feeling both hungry and caffeine deprived. What all this was really about was venturing outside my comfort zone. Tango is already this ambivalent way-station of familiarity and strangeness in that I know the dance but each place has its own sensibility and social codes. I prefer to know the way of the land and its customs but I also concede that once in a while, I have to step a bit further out lest I get too comfortable.

I found the street where *Café Lima* was situated and it was narrow and busy street, almost a condensed strip of Broadway but instead of theatres it was comprised of congested retail stores. Stores stacked on stores and squished beside more stores were my first impression. There were dress and shoe shops, hat stores, bridal shops, electronics and more. I'd never seen such a hodge-podge. The street itself, being so tight made it so you could almost stand in the middle of it, span out your arms and touch the store-fronts on both sides. Where on earth would a tango place be in this land of materialism?

I re-checked the address several times and finally found a tiny, dark door almost hidden behind a huge archway. I parked and ventured near the door, still dubious. Just as I would have turned away, a woman manifested out of the shadows. Wearing strategically fashion-ripped tango clothes, smoking a cigarette in a retro burgundy cigarette holder, she motioned with some of the smoke curls and a careless flex of her hand. "*C'est en haut'* (it's upstairs"). No need to ask how she knew what I was there for; tango people know other tango people. Relieved to know I was in the right place I went up the shadowy swirl of steps, inhaling old dark maple wood stairs, with a patina of time and scuff marks, and slight traces of mildew and smoke. I opened the door at the top of the stairs and fell into a tango portal. Crossing from the stair-top (it would be a stretch to call it a landing) I tumbled into the barely lit room. The bar was immediately on my right while red sofas and black leather seats, coated the sides of a long room with its slick wood dancing floor. Couples were moving, listing, leaning, swaying and turning to barely audible music. On the walls were vintage photos of Gardel, Di Sarli and d'Arienzo and old tango LP's; the dense scent of dark amber and spice perfume, aftershave, beer and red wine was thick in the air.

The place was jammed packed! There was heat, vibrant splashes of dresses all set against Argentinian hospitality. *This* was a tango place as tango had been when I first started, when the venues were sketchy and interesting, where I never knew a soul but where my appetite for adventure was stronger than my worry about being asked to dance. It was tango as I loved it best: uncharted, non-conformist and out of an era long past.

I barely got my shoes on and wonders of wonders, due to a happy shortage of women followers, I was asked to dance immediately by a brawny, West Indian man who told me he was from Grenada and his name was Peggy. "Peggy" was as hefty a Peggy as one could ever meet and he led beautifully! After him I danced with several other good leaders. Each one was different, kind, and competent. I was so happy to be back in the groove and all in all, it was a welcoming reception.

I stayed until one am and left when I'd had my fill of dances, dancers, and dance styles. As I closed the door, I closed the gateway between the world of music and its brilliant shades of orange and smoke and crossed back over to the default world. I minced my way to my car that waited patiently like a sturdy pack pony. It was at the ready to ferry me home to the suburbs where the only tango is at the *Arthur Murray* studio in the strip mall or *Dancing with the Stars.*

Driving away from *Café Lima* I was happy to know it was there and I could always find a new adventure simply by driving to a new place, navigating unfamiliar streets in service to finding a fresh new dance floor and unusual suspects. As the saying goes, it keeps you on your toes.

Many of us might claim we need safety and familiarity but we also all need something unpredictable and strange. Tango places, like *Café Lima,* should never been too slick or fancy. May these places also always have brawny men with unexpected names like *Peggy* poised to whisk you into an interlude that starts on the ground and ends in mid-air and brings you back to start all over again?

INTERLUDE

FOUR SEASONS OF TANGO: SPRING TANGO PRIMAVERA AND THE WARM-UP GUYS

After a long winter, spring finally comes. I may or may not have managed to do a lot of winter tango. Battling the early sunsets, cold air, snow-stuck streets and parking might have dampened my tango forays. But then it's April and that lightness of a new season has me thinking about new tango shoes, new flowery tops and finding a class I can sink my teeth into. I probably a good eight weeks of a *vals* or *milonga* tango to pep me up. But I'm rusty and need to get up to speed for the new season. And that is where thoughts turn to my loyal leads: the tango warm-up guys.

If you're going to go the distance at tango, you'll always need some warm-up guys. Who or what are the warm-up guys? The warm-up men (or leaders or people of any gender who lead) are the men who I know and are familiar, decent, and reliable leaders who keep me on my toes but aren't too intimidating. They are safe bets or safe leads and most often, they are the lovely fellows I'm currently in a class with and the people I'm most comfortable dancing with. As a rule you can anticipate the people you dance with at least once a week in a class will can also be relief on (almost) to dance with you at a practica.

Warm-up guys are the get-back-into-the-swim guys. These are the ones you get your tango feet wet with before you go after bigger game. I know it sounds unkind or overtly strategic, i.e. almost like these men are appetizers before the main event but they are easy-going men you can count on. If there's any chemistry, it's usually or more often about mutual ability and personality. That said, I've learned two things concerning the warm-up guys.

One is that this ploy (and I hesitate to call it a ploy) is a two way street. For some other guy, no doubt, someone I would term more challenging game (i.e. more advanced and/or with some lurking chemistry), 'I" am the 'warm up girl'. So that's a humbling context.

The second thing is this: *even* a warm up guy can say *no* to you and/or turn on the charm. When a warm-up guy refuses to dance with you, it's not a good thing but you get over it. It's also not to say that you can't ask *them* to dance. It's more a matter of on the occasions they don't seek you out as they customarily do you'll feel rejected. You might smile, say hello and make all sorts of yes/please ask me to dance/eye antics and they simply choose not to ask you. The first few times this happened to me was disconcerting. *Even Joseph,* you say to yourself. *Even Joseph* won't ask me? Then you realize again that in tango, as in life, the power shifts to and fro every other day. There's nothing you can count on save the fact that there's nothing you can count on. Unreliability is the only sure thing; limbo is terra firma. In this strange land no one holds all the cards, all the time.

You'd also, if you're given to believing in stereotypes, conclude that it'd be prettier, younger women that rule the roost but that's not always do. At one tango studio I frequent there's a woman who's deep into her 70's. She's very attractive and always exceptionally well-dressed but she's simply not a great dancer as she tends to back lead or lean and talks throughout dancing. But more to the point, she's not particularly a warm or engaging person. I've experienced her as bitter on more than one occasion and plainly rude on others – *to everyone* in fact. Yet I've observed so many times where she dominates the dance floor and is asked to dance repeatedly while the rest of the female flock sits. That's oddly reassuring because it says to me: we never know what the asker is looking for in a dance partner. You can't assume anything in this world that makes up its own rules only to break them as per its discretion or whim. If this woman is dancing so often (and with the best leaders and handsomest men) then you can't conclude, *well the others are prettier or better or nicer or friendlier so that is why they dance more* because a) this isn't the case and b) because there is no rhyme or reason.

I've learned to treat my warm up guys with respect. Knowing at any given time, I'm also a warm-up act and/or the warm-up guys can reassert their real estate value. All this takes is a cool mood or an evening when the male leader ranks are especially lean or your own impatience to be asked to dance has your warm-up guys hunting others. So is always a good thing.

The truth is there's ***no*** such thing as a *warm-up* guy. There are simply people who you're always compatible with, who accept you as you are and welcome you to an afternoon or evening of tango like an old friend. For that, I am always grateful to these partners and I hope I offer that back in kind to them or anyone else.

CHAPTER NINETEEN

CLOSE EMBRACE TANGO AND THE MAGIC OF CAESAR

It's graduation night at tango - well, in a fashion. For those of us who've danced tango in excess of three years or umpteen courses we're now in a new session called *Close Embrace.* I'm so in! In French they call it *Style de Rapprochement* which sounds even more intriguing. It means: close dancing or in the case of tango: even closer dancing.

When you begin tango, you're taught to use the default or open position of the dance stance or what is more of a classic ballroom dance look. You hold the man's bicep with your left hand; you allow him to clasp your right hand and that is held outward, mid-way between the torsos of the woman and her partner. Ballroom people talk a lot about creating a frame for the woman and I agree that the whole notion of *frame* is lovely, sedate, classic and graceful. But *close embrace* is another beast entirely and it's irresistible. Given the choice of being charmingly 'framed' or being warmly embraced it's no contest.

How does *close embrace* work? You loop your left arm around the man's neck or more often the middle of his back but in essence whatever you do with your arms results in you being laminated to his torso, belly to belly like one fused being. If you can't manage your arm around his neck (he's much taller than you) or the middle of his back you can snake your left hand as far around their left shoulder blade and beyond as possible. However you get there, the goal is to be in a seamless embrace. No matter how you style it, mechanically-speaking 'close embrace (aka how people in tango dance by default) takes confidence and a finesse. On some nights both are out of my reach. On other nights it's the most natural away to dance; you feel protected and in another world. *Close embrace* is generally easier to follow since the lead comes more from the man's chest. You only release when doing certain steps which demand some space to maneuver.

Close embrace is actually how tango is *meant* to be danced or at least what came before *salon-style* tango with the *Milonguero*-style tango. It can be more challenging because it takes some extra social confidence or simply because there are steps that make you step out a bit of the close embrace to allow for a turn or *oucho*. Overall it looks more sinuous and for some musical pieces, it's also less stilted.

My first partner in *Close Embrace* class was Caesar who's about 5'9", long, shiny, black hair like Zorro, lean over-all but expectantly broad-shouldered, together with an impassive expression and little eye contact. Caesar dances like a lion stalking prey. Technically he's simply a superb and well-skilled dancer but he's also innately lyrical so dancing with him becomes like a voyage to another land on a magic carpet. Between dances however, he's a bit frosty and certainly impassive. When the music starts again he sweeps me back and our conspiracy of uneasy intimacy that only exists by virtue of the fact that we share it between us and not the outside world. It's also because it's in such sharp contrast to his way-of-being when there's no dancing and music going on.

Much is made about women who like sensitive men and I appreciate sensitive *people* in general. But once in a while, you meet a man who enjoys or just is a man in somewhat old-fashioned terms. We're not talking Stanley Kowalski bellowing at Stella but just about this sort of masculinity which is just about gone these days (and some say good riddance but that's a whole other subject). As poised as the men of tango generally are, Caesar has an 'it' factor. Of course, this is all politically incorrect or has lost its meaning, given that masculinity is as diverse and political a subject as femininity. Granted there are many ways of being masculine from one end of the spectrum to another and given that even the term *masculine* as well as *feminine* might be a social artifice. But in any dictionary meaning of *macho*, Caesar is *a lot* of guy.

He's a contender for first place because he reaches all the right notes and it's like we speak the same dialect of a lost language. No matter what he doles out to me in steps, complications, turns, different pacing, dramatic pauses or sweeps, subtle nuances, everything but overhead lifts, I'm able to respond without a single falter. I stick to him like glue or like Ruth: whither he goeth, I go. It's like being a violin and finally the right musician picks you up, plays you as *you* like to be played and instinctively chooses your own favorite melody in your own favorite key. I'm amazed Caesar isn't impressed but he gives no indication of anything. It's like this incredible match-up happens every day. But this is the thing: the *minute* the music ends, he releases me like spring lock and physically distances himself as if nothing happened.

He could have been hawking *Cutco* knives because there's absolutely no clue that something magical just occurred. Maybe it *was* ordinary dancing with exceptional connection. Either way, I'm always baffled. Not even a nod afterwards!

I've often heard that when men reveal themselves, say in an intimate moment if this results in a vulnerable feeling, they might regroup by appearing cool. I wonder if tango has this same impact on the men in it. The first time this i.e. Caesar seemed impassive or unmoved after a great dance, I was crest-fallen. A definite frost moved in where heat so recently radiated. It was always such a contrast to the mutual intimacy of the dance and a true let-down to think he didn't notice a thing.

Over time I began to resent how he almost cast me off after each dance but I decided this is the price of admission. So I trained myself to be still and indifferent after dances. I would coolly disentangle myself by brushing my skirt for imaginary lint, and checking the back of my shoulder as if to discover a bird perched there that was a mindless, curious happenstance. If the *it-factor* of tango or I was nothing then I too could feign neutrality and provide a finishing touch of ice versus sun.

I became quicker at leaving his embrace before he could and adept at appearing just a bit colder than him. My reward one night was that he asked me if everything was alright and I said *yes, of course and thank you* and walked away, stopping to re-tie my shoe strap (unnecessarily) for emphasis. In retrospect maybe my expectations were too high. I'm not sure what I wanted really from him but sense of appreciation might had been nice so I would know I wasn't in the experience alone.

As time has gone on, I wonder if I misread something but that juxtaposition of perfect connection and then coolness always baffled me. I suppose people, especially tango people have their quirks. If you need any sort of personal validation or a mirror image of your best self, tango might not be the place to seek it out.

Since that class, on the occasions I've wound up with Caesar in class situation during a partner exchange I've maintained the *sang froid*. With Peter my *Vals* tango partner I am sweet and demure because *he's* so kind and demure. With Hugo, I'm an irritated Eliza Doolittle with Henry Higgins or Katherine the Shrew. After dancing with Hugo I feel like handing him my resume or my notice.

But with Caesar, I'm the least recognizable to others and yet the most 'me' I ever get to be. With him, I'm the version that no one who knows me best would recognize but the person I like the best – incredibly alive, expressive, not self-conscious and free to create.

And this business with Caesar, looking and seeming cool when I feel anything but? I've actually learned to like being quieter and less emotional. It's like a vacation from myself. But it's not authentic and it takes work even while it serves because it's not me. You can't give more than you're getting or you'll feel daft.

I also think about the comparisons of open position versus *close embrace* tango. There's a real feeling of acceptance in *close embrace.* Both dancers can feel their hearts beating, the breath work, the body warmth, the fragrance of each other, the tension or lack of tension as you follow or flow. There's no place to hide but you do forget about it all as you dance and focus on your steps and the music. Let me just add that I think that unique listening may very well be the new era of true eroticism in the 21st century. That listening or attunement with another person is what makes tango so intimate. The good news and bad news is tango *is* just a dance and dances end. Most of who you are by default or necessity is what continues after you leave the dance floor and walk back into your life. The same is true for the partner you danced with. Still, after each dance and stranger you've shared it with, you're forever altered ....if just a bit.

CHAPTER TWENTY

THE SCENT OF TANGO

(He inhales)

"Fleurs de Rocaille"

"Yes".

"Flowers from a brook"

"That's right".

"Well, Miss Downes, I'll know where to find you"

(Al Pacino, as Colonel Slade from the film, Scent of a Woman)

As a professional chef fragrance is inherently vitally important to me but it's even more primordial to me as a person. In the kitchen, creating recipes for my cookbooks, it's all about that bouquet of cinnamon, lemon, orange, chocolate, berries and vanilla that drifts in a cloud of baking bread, scones, cakes and cookies. Outside the kitchen, I leave most of the foodie scents behind or enjoy them in toiletries and perfumes. I've long collected perfumes and also have a storehouse of incense, essential oils and magic elixirs to revive body and soul. Nothing makes me happier than smelling a new perfume or finding a new oil of bergamot or just inhaling roses in spring for that matter.

It's not surprising then as a tango woman, scent has on occasion, upstaged the dance itself. How could it not? Someone's scent easily rivals touch for a first impression.
Scent is both aesthetic and sensual and innately powerful. It's an olfactory elixir of time and human history with a wing span that embraces centuries. Scent is probably the most connective chord of the mind, body and soul. It is primal – tethered to our very survival instincts and yet, in more refined contexts it's no less visceral, as light, romantic and memorable as your first kiss. Like music, scent rarely encounters indifference. Like love, it touches us all and like life itself, scent is the very breath we take.

Scent is the last of our five senses to go or otherwise diminish as we age. It's our sensory GPS, an early warning system that cautions us of danger, forecasts pleasure, signals either a gourmet meal or poison, tainted water or the exalted inhalations of spring first lilacs. A simple scent in the air tells us when we are home, and when we are in a strange land, and when the seasons, both inner and outer, are changing.

Regardless of the specific scent, be it frying onions, mud or *Chanel No 5*, something profound and emotional is stirred when you smell things. It could be good or off-putting but there's a visceral response. More than any other sense, more than the melody line of a favorite song of a lost love, scent has that ability to bring a distant time and forgotten place in your life forward to the present moment. One whiff and it's suddenly on the front doorstep of your consciousness. It's may be an artifact from the past but in an instant, heralded in on a swath of emotions and mood, it becomes your indelible present. With one breath, you're transported and that singular, unexpected perfume of your history becomes a fragrant time machine.

Those in the medical sciences as well as aroma therapists and holistic practitioners, who use scent therapeutically, have long been aware that the accuracy of our memories increases ten-fold when scent accompanies the intellectual reverie. More recently, physicists have discovered that different scents smell different *not* because the scent molecules are *shaped* differently but because they each have a *different vibration or energy*, as well as electromagnetic field which goes a long way as the science underlying why essential oils heal, and perfumes engage the spirit, igniting a flood of romantic response.

How does scent relate to my tango life?

So what's the big deal about tango and scent? Well, there are people who dance poorly but they smell so great that I don't care and I tend to think their dancing is better than it is *simply* because they are a pleasure to be close to! There are people (men, in my case) who have this aura of fragrance that enhances the dancing. It could be *Gucci*, fresh laundry or soap or clean sweat, but it's something I am happy to tuck myself into and makes me remember those dances and look forward to more.

I take great care in choosing the scents I wear to tango. Often I don't opt for anything other than plain soap and water because not everyone appreciates perfume or a specific perfume and it's only solicitous to factor that in especially in this day and age when even fragrance is part of cancel culture. But no one wants to be swamped in a heavy perfume or cologne of someone else.

When I *do* wear one of my perfumes, I usually only wear it on my left side so that no one dancing with me is subjected to too much of it. I also choose things that are light like a green tea scent (*Green Tea* by *Bylvari* is perfect) or crowd-pleasing appealing like vanilla or sandalwood oil. Big*elow Apothecaries* makes gorgeous vanilla oil as does Kuramba but so many mainstream or designer scents, especially *Guerlain*, hold anchoring notes of vanilla.

Years ago, my scent-of-the-day was the classic *Hanae Mori EDP* which had just launched. I wore it to tango class the very day I bought it. My default partner at the time, Hugo and I, were not a great match and after a while, there was barely cordiality between us. It was a random pairing – we had inherited each other – and neither of us would quit each other for whatever reason. To say we didn't have dance chemistry is an understatement. To be frank I found him truculent and prickly and I felt very unwelcome in his embrace.

The really unfortunate part of Hugo is that he was hard on himself and therefore hard on those around him. So my trust only goes as far as his acceptance of himself which is limited. I never felt that for him I am a good thing. It's more like we are both struggling like the two beggars like that hapless pair on the Tarot card (the couple shown outside a Church window). Hugo does have a bit of a sense of humor which helps but in my heart of hearts I think he was rather lonely. He lost his father between two tango sessions, a remote, high achieving man he idolized. I went to the commemorative service which was held at a university since his father was a renowned scholar there. It was a big deal but on a good note, since it was uncomfortable for me to be there (I only went to be solicitous) there were hundreds of people in attendance. So Hugo who's always glum and stern was especially so in those days. My empathy notwithstanding, to be frank, he was just ornery. I've danced with him for three years and have come to conclude that he and I are like oil and water or like flowers and cement. I am poetry; he is the terse rules of grammar. I am ad-libbed music and he is the rigidity of Mozart. We simply never dance well so we certainly don't make music together; that's for sure.

In every class that I danced with him, he blamed any mis-step on me and quite vocally or with a stream of titches of the tongue. Every too-fast turn that upset my equilibrium, I blamed on him although I never vocalized it. We smiled at each on in exasperated moments with barely concealed irritation, trying to be polite but each one thinking the other one was impossible. But then one day, I came to class wearing the *Hanae Morie* eau du parfum.

Hanae Morie smells like berries in a forest with touches of fir trees and sunlight. It's exceptional. Hugo opened his embrace and took me in his arms for the warm-up. And guess what? He immediately wilted; his knees actually buckled. *What's wrong,* I asked. He answered: *what are you wearing? My god, that scent! It's unbelievably beautiful.*

Hurray I thought! Unwittingly I had conquered the beast. He has his kryptonite and that potion in this case is my perfume that smells like berries in a dew-laced forest, redolent of roses, cedar and sandalwood and romantic promise. *That's* the power of a scent. It even felled Hugo.

I'd like to say that after that moment we became an amical and high performance partnership but the following week, when I returned wearing Elizabeth Arden's *Green Tea* eau du parfum the magic had evaporated. The armistice was clearly over and Hugo was back to be hyper-critical and clucking with his tongue at every *ocho* or *boleo.* But in that one moment the week before, a scented surrender as it were, enabled me to see the chink in Hugo's armour. He wasn't totally immune or maybe it was that he missed his father and was vulnerable. We will never know.

Scent is a center post in my life and choosing a scent for tango is a joy to consider and just another level of your whole dance experience. All this considered, if the dance chemistry is really off, and a baseline humanity or gallantry is also missing, no amount of *Eau Savage, Hanae Morie* or the iconic *Fleurs de Rocailles* is going to fix it.

THE FOUR SEASONS OF TANGO: SUMMER SUMMER TANGO OR TANGO AL FRESCO

After spring of course, comes summer and nothing is as sublime as the balmy tango of summer. The sun sets later and the air is mellow as nature sets a stage for two precious months of dance outdoors. Summer tango implies tango-in-the-park or tango in some-green-and-concreate downtown nook in some gentrified part of the city. No matter where it is, it's an indescribable experience. If you were to lasso one of life's perfect moments it would probably be this one: dancing outdoors, perhaps in a gazebo, with the heady perfume of florals and verdant shrubbery, as the stars gaze down, spotlighting you and the other dancers in the gentle darkness of an early summer evening. It is magnificent, priceless and it's free to boot. *Tango al fresco* also, much like a Sunday afternoon practica, is an informal occasion which tends to draw out interesting people you're less familiar with and there are more possibilities to dance.

Summer tango begins around seven pm although there is often mid-afternoon tango to be found. Traditionally a free introductory lesson is offered to tango newbies or people strolling in the park who might impulsively decide to stop being a life-bystander, take a leap and try it. There's no cost after all and a beginner lesson is literally a walk in the park and relatively risk free. It's not *Cirque du Soleil* stuff and you can have those proverbial two left feet and still succeed. Tango studios who host the in-the-park events also hope that some percentage of free customers convert into a paying new students for the studio or as word-of-mouth advertisers for tango. How better to open up this clandestine world than to take it outdoors in public?

That first half-hour the dance floor is split between the slightly struggling tango neophytes, as they delicately stumble their way through those first basic steps. Then familiar tango faces and more veteran dancers stroll in, much like a quietly happening flash dance mob assembling, onto the dance floor. Seeing anyone you know from a tango studio or the confines of your tango class in the wild of a summer park is like seeing a whole new person. In keeping with the tango world, they may or may not acknowledge you even if they know you well. In fact, on some occasions, even if they are your default tango partner they may walk by you with a blank look. It sounds ridiculous and off-putting but by this point, if you've been in tango even a short while, you get used to it.

In some ways as someone walks into a tango event they are cruising and surveying the possibilities and laying out their dance strategy. If they acknowledge you (like a normal person would) then they might feel obliged to commit and dance with you and honestly or sadly, people are picky and they wait to see what the offerings are as the sun begins its slow descent. They may or may not ask you to dance on that night or upcoming. Of course you can always ask them but most often the ratio of male leaders to female followers is skewed and whereas that not caution someone else, it does make me prefer to wait than risk a no. at least in that venue. Wait, hold up, I can the detractors saying: *but why wait to be asked to dance?*

I have my theories and an evolving rule book.

First of all, when there are three-to-one or worse odds of male leaders to female followers and therefore men have their choice, I prefer to wait to be asked. Then I know for sure that person chose me. Of course, I *could* choose to be more assertive and invite a leader to dance with me but when the odds are that stacked, it's not appealing to me. Depending on my mood (and confidence) and geography (how far the walk from the person I asked is and the walk back to my seat or perch) I might find it more challenge than I'm up for. If I do ask on such evenings, I tend to wait near till the end so that I can scurry home quickly afterwards if it's a bust and I tend to have more moxy at the end of a tango evening. I'm *not* saying this is how everyone approaches tango but it is, for now, how I do it. In tango, as in life, you need to learn to honor yourself.

But here's another thing about tango in the park. If a night goes well, it's breath-taking and you're so grateful to be healthy and dancing this beautiful, timeless dance with the moon as your witness. If it goes a little less well, well then you're still healthy and able to dance which is a blessing. Then on the way home, the night still being young, you can stay out or grab a coffee at an outdoor café, read a book and celebrate life. In effect, you've taken yourself out for an excursion, avoided *Netflix* and extended summer by being an after-hours participant of it. Tango-in-the-park on a perfect July night is a perfect excuse to get you outside and living up every last ounce of a summer's day warmth.

Time passes quickly in warmer months and pretty soon August seeps in and you can feel things wind down. The air follows suit with coolness; multi-colored leaves dust the park where you danced a few weeks prior. You begin checking the tango schools' schedules online to see what you register for. You yourself will be in a different headspace, as September cues another sort of life in all of us. Still, as you happen to drive by the area you might see the shadow ghosts of dancers, moving to silent music, at the behest of your own memory. But in reality, what was so lively in summer is now simply an abandoned green space. The water fountains are closed, the ground is taut and chilled; a few dog walkers and their pets tramp through what was the dance floor. Another season moves in and the park waits for the first snow.

CHAPTER TWENTY-ONE

THE ART AND MYTH OF LETTING GO

Wherever you turn in life they talk about the virtues of letting go. *Just let go – release and flow.* As if it was easy. Sometimes although, somewhat rarely in life it is possible to let go but in tango, not so much.

We were in class and paused between new steps when Tomás, our teacher for *Close Embrace Tango*, suddenly launched into a random tango riff. It's that thing tango teacher do that I love where they suddenly share an insight about how and why tango is how it is, via the filter of their vision and experience. It's part of our a collective, unceasing effort to define yet another undefinable nuance of this dance we love so much.

"Ever notice how sometimes you dance with a woman and all is going well? The music, the connection, the flow, the steps? And you almost forget yourself?" Tomás asks.

All of us nod. We know exactly what he means. Of course we do. We are *always* reaching for that moment with that perfect stranger. In tango, it's a one-time thing or it's terminal.

Tomás forgets he is teaching steps and the class minutes are ticking away. He wanders more into that place we all think about but rarely voice or share with each other. His voice changes, his posture wilts as he relaxes into a conversational mode. We lean back on the columns, the walls, each other; some of us sit down for a moment. We love where these conversations go.

"And then....in that moment where the woman forgets herself. She lends herself to the man and the dance. Without warning – in that place of....bliss? The steps either go awry of she becomes like dead weight. In that moment, she forgets to hold herself up, to remember she is a separate person and has a responsibility to be aware and listen, and follow. And then it's like dragging her. It is not so romantic at this point and it becomes so quickly, simply: bad tango'

I know what he means because as a follower, I've been there; I *always* want to let go. Who wouldn't? To fall in love for those precious minutes, to fly and float on air and be fantastic and not think, not be in your head? Just *be there* in tango land with some guy you convince yourself could be more than he is or other than your rational brain has already figured out. It takes but a few good sequences, smooth steps and an accordance to music you like. You decide you like his scent and his lead and the way his body molds to yours. You decide to go on a little romance or at least a fantasy or just enjoy it disproportionately.

But before you take that leap, the rules of tango step in and tango is a hard mistress. She reminds you to hold your head and your body both up and upright and support yourself. You can't just flop on someone else and lean your full weight onto them. You can't forget where you are and you don't get the freedom to fall in love and be weightless because tango – like love and life – always features this gravity thing.

This gravity thing is the terra firma of reality and the realization that you are alone in tango and probably just as often, alone in life. That's why this illusion of flying with some stranger is so riveting because for three minutes or less, the gravity thing disappears. So you forget and try and surrender to a long-term thing, even knowing what you know and inevitably, you'll fall back to earth with a thud. Worse, you can even pull someone else down on the way.

Tango is so duplicitous. Along with the seduction it has there's also this F-you elegance and autonomy that is only vaguely veiled in seduction and charm. Sometimes it's a war out there.

It all reminds me think of that D.H. Lawrence *Sons and Lovers* scene wherein the two lovers drown in the reservoir and are found clutched in a final embrace of love and death. *She killed him* says one by-stander to another, as in: she dragged him down to the depths. In being so clutchy, she drowned them both.

Tango with its ground rule about but not *quite* letting go has also taught me to fall in love in measured amounts. I have to remember when the one I love steps away or doesn't reciprocate that I still have a life I love. I am *still* an entity entirely onto itself. In that way, when the one I love beckons again and makes space I can walk back upright, balanced and whole.

It's been awhile since I've taken a class with Tomás but I still remember his words. Perhaps it's just outside of tango that I seem to forget or *outside* of tango that this business of letting go is one of life's better philosophies. In bread baking, the new technique is *all* about leaving the bread alone. Less touch, less kneading, more rise, more rest equals better bread. You cannot flog things or otherwise redirect the river and if you just leave the bread (and all else alone) it all works out and there's flow. And more than flow, the other good news is on the other side of this letting go and falling, one can themselves again: whole and separate and still, more than enough woman or *person* to try it all over again.

Letting go in tango is the one lesson *O* Magazine cannot teach you and one of the many lessons tango, bread and life has taught me best. I've learned this by almost drowning in the vortex of passion and now keep back just a little bit so I can recoup – no matter where I am. It's wonderful to have wings and fly; it's a bit more wonderful to land on your feet, on earth, where you live.

Maybe you can't give all of yourself to love any more than you can give all of yourself to tango. It works just as well when I'm not engaged in some personal romance and instead, life is my default partner. In those times, I've learned to go with the tides of the day and not cling to any piece of human weather which is far more mercurial.

CHAPTER TWENTY-TWO

THE PRODIGAL DANCER RETURNS OR POST PANDEMIC TANGO

When and *how* to return to tango? This is the question tango dancers (dancers in general) world-wide have wondered since the pandemic began. The pandemic was a game changer and there's still one contagion or another around these days. How can tango be safe again 'when you're out together dancing cheek to cheek"?

When I took my last tango class just before the very beginning of the brunt of Covid the tango studios had begun to close anyway, complying with the circumstances and dictates of the virus and the government. Suddenly, there was a new playbook for anything to do with people gathering whether it was in a grocery store or worse on the dance floor. The dance world was one of the hardest hit stratus of all things social. But if I'm being honest, I was also somewhat disenchanted just before Covid gave me an excuse to take a break.

Anyone who stays the course in tango experiences this or occasional times of they love it a bit less. The can be a scarcity of partners at your level or a shortage of partners altogether or you don't get asked to dance as much. You go from studio to studio, different days and times or take special sessions with visiting tango teachers. You try to recapture that magic. But it's like wet flint that simply won't ignite, not even a spark. Each time you winnow down into these fallow times you wonder if that is indeed, the end of your tango life. The magic dwindles and in its place there's a tango malaise which you try hard not to see not because you can't take a break but what if it's not a break but the new shape of the inner terrain of you? One dips in and out of one's dance life for many reasons and this thing about germs, in context of a close-dance, is a bit more problematic but the return for me was inevitable.

As the enforced sabbatical went on (and like many of us, I took Zoom tango classes and networked worldwide in tango conversations with other lonely dancers) I began to sincerely miss it. Even the people that I never danced with – strange but true; I missed them too! I realized that as long as I'm breathing, it will always be too early in the day to leave tango.

As the years go by, I've only come to see I have many tango miles left in me. When missing tango turned to a true longing, the externals got safer to deal with and so I have made my way back.

Tango One: An encore, Beginners Class Revisited

Last night I stepped onto the tango dance floor for the first time in three years. I had wobbly, Bambi-like legs that clearly signalled the length of time I'd been absent from tango. No amount of at-home practise with a broomstick as a partner can make up for real life, partner dancing. Even though I chose my lowest-heeled, most worn-in tango shoes that are as comfortable as slippers my balance was still questionable – nothing to rely on but I'm certain I wasn't alone in that. So many of us, the majority in fact, have been away from tango for a long time and are rusty. That's hardly a concern – because now amid the entrails of an older tango community there's a fresher one that's rebuilding itself. We're all glad to be back a group of old and new trickle in.

Happily (at least for me), everyone was obliged to wear a mask (kindly provided at the reception area) which is the only way I could return to tango given the evidence that the pandemic isn't quite over. But finally, on that rainy Monday night in early fall, where the mist from the black streets outside the studio wafted a phantom fog, I strapped on my shoes. In seconds there I was again as if I'd never left, back in tango again gliding into a new person's embrace. A million sighs mixed with nervousness broke forth inside me.

There was trepidation: would I remember the steps or how to follow? What would it be liked to be held by a new stranger when I'd been away so long? Could anyone hear my heart beating?

Probably not because the telltale heart sound was drown out, I am sure, by everyone else's beating hearts. When tango is new or new again, it's impossible to pretend to be casual but one does. Guess what? It was perfect - clumsy, rusty, familiar and still perfect! It was almost as if I never left but it was different and in so many good ways.

For starters, it was a brilliant idea to go back to the beginner level of tango. My reasoning was a few-fold.

By choosing to begin all over again I could practise basics and build up my dancing muscle, fluidity and confidence. I also envisioned a whole new fleet of newcomers to re-experience tango again for the first time and I was so right to do that! Vis a vis the mechanics it gives you more runway to catch up on all that you've lost. But you're also dancing with fresh horses that are all energy, all smiles and sport a lack of jadedness.

The expectations on a veteran but-out-of-shape tango dancer are low to nil, not that anyone really can suspect I'm a well-practiced dancer especially as I am a follower. That means I'm responding versus leading or initiating and that for me is both easier and instinctive. There's also a tacit lack of judgement in a beginner class because we're all either new to tango and/or new to each other. There are tango virgins and born-again tango virgins and no one can tell the difference which makes it a beautifully equalizing experience. Big bonus? I don't recognize (albeit everyone is masked) anyone in the class. Gone are all the usual suspects I know too well and know me too well. I have no identity here and I can be anyone I like or perhaps for once 100% myself.

Thrillingly, it was a large class of forty or twenty couples. I looked around and noticed of the ten women, only three wore traditional tango shoes or even character dance shoes. Everyone else wore either stocking-feet, Nike, Birkenstock, cowboy boots and one had bare feet. Not *one* woman was in a skirt or dress; most wore what I call Gumby pants (wide, high-wasted jeans) or overalls with one strap down. Overall, the vibe was street-wear and a distinctly non-binary. The world had changed and tango, always a forecaster of what's going on socially, was fully clad in that change. Years ago, when I began tango, everyone wore some version of black and the women wore rather sexy, slinky things and even practise shoes had impressive height to them. By comparison, this group was far more laid-back than all the previous groups and the anything goes approach was fresh and welcoming and underscored an easy-going, democratic approach to somewhat-too-serious tango. The emphasis was on having fun, connecting and mostly learning and all of us starting in the same boat. There was that tiny but evident excitement in the air - the wee bit of tingle that all beginnings feature. It's probably my favorite part of both tango and life itself: beginnings : where *everything* good is still possible or where there are just endless possibilities of how things will go.

I love my new class which is essentially beginner level. It's a class of novices who've been in tango barely six weeks but here we're all together in a great big equalized dance pen. I'm anonymous to this group and they are to me; I feel both welcoming and welcomed back. I'm delighted with my partner called Nathanial but have no idea of what he really looks like as he, like everyone else, is masked. Nathanial is quiet with a gray-streaked wispy pony-tail. Quiet or not, each week he grows more confident but is innately solicitous.

I love dressing up again, choosing a new perfume to wear and enjoy the sounds of people in a social setting, so missing from the quarantine world we're all coming off of.

Many veteran tango people are returning these days although we've lost many via these strange years. But there are many newbies who evidently decided that when they *could* do so, they would make their way to a dance class. Some went to *salsa* or Western line dancing, Contra, Ballroom and West Coast Swing. And some, my new tribe of other brave souls, geeked up for as much connection as the world could offer them ended up here at tango with me.

At tango there is always there to catch and hold you, to lead you or let you lead them. Tango is a place where few or absolutely no one may know your name or what you do but they know exactly what you feel like, move and breathe like. I think that's even better Intel.

This is a place where the lights are dim but the people are bright and lit up inside. Here, you're free to be *more* of who you really are or craving to be. Here you can finally be seen. And once seen you cannot go back to *where* you were or *how* you were. It's worth the price of admission.

CHAPTER TWENTY THREE

FOREVER TANGO

I've been in love with tango so long that I just can't remember a time when I didn't even know what tango was. I certainly don't remember who *I* was before it.

What I *do* remember, as clear as etchings on the Rosetta stone, are those moments leading just prior to opening the door to that first tango class. Unlike most people, I didn't even have any preconceived tango notions, i.e. swooning lovers with roses in their teeth or a vision of Al Pacino doing a tango in *Scent of a Woman*. In whatever space the reality of my tango now resides, there was nothing. I must have been saving room for it.

So much time has passed since I saw a print newspaper ad that said "*Free Introduction Class to Tango'* and felt compelled to go. It was only four days into the separation that has led to the only divorce I hope to experience. I was in such pain that the very blood in my body cracked and howled. Whatever made me think tango would be the tonic? But tango must be quite wise because here I am now a: woman deep into the fall of her life, still dressing in crushed velvet and risking snow storms to get to that room where there is a floor but no ceiling and the possibility of experiencing the most extraordinary connection a human being can dream of on this earth.

The first time I took my first tango class, full of trepidation and wanting to flee from the moment I parked my car and went up the narrow stairway step to the sparse, warehouse tango studio, I was already smitten by a force larger than life. Somehow in my bones, *I knew.* This was a home I missed and never experienced. Tango has claimed a third of my life and it's my prayer, among many but certainly one of my major prayers that one day I may be honored to say that over half my life has had tango in it. Anyone should be so lucky. Anyone should be so blessed.

I've been to many other dance venues and they are all special and unique. But among other things, mostly what tango people want is that connection where every single part, *every* single cell, *every* inch of their mind/body/spirit gets met. They will dance a million miles, over and over, on the same quarter acres of dance floor, to get there. When they do, they are satiated for a spell and then the drum beat of that hunger begins all over again. That is what makes tango a one-off or terminal. Anyone discovers, even while fluttery and nervous in that first dance class, what it *can* be for them. Whatever that is will also change just like the other seasons as you yourself as your morph in your abilities, moods, and personal evolutions.

The other night at a tango soiree, I sat and waited to dance. I saw the other women: younger, older, slim, not slim, and more coy or less expectant, be led to the dance floor. It was early but I was not yet asked to dance and I wasn't in a mood to ask someone myself. Yes, I now ask men to dance. To come to tango means you take a risk of being the forgotten swan *or* belle of the ball or the corps du ballet or all of those things. There is no rhyme or reason to any of it, as it infolds, on any given night. There is neither app nor emoji that that allows you to forgo the experience of waiting to be asked which is what makes tango in the new millennium still feel like the world, circa 1930.

But then a mysterious and wild-looking, handsome unknown man who, until then was part of the wallpaper, came into my view. He took form, arising from the wallpaper into relief and dimension. He nodded to me from over thirty meters away in the dimness of the dance floor perimeter. I nodded back. That nod is called a *cabeceo* and when both people nod there is an agreement to dance together.

I walked to the dance floor; the mystery man walked the greater distance to meet me. Inches apart, we faced each other before the music started. That alone takes a poise most people can't image and will never have. He raised his hand and captured my right hand; his other arm encircled my waist and then we took those first tentative steps. I was not disappointed.

I'm a 'save the best for last' girl and he was very much worth the preamble of missed, mediocre dances. He was balletic, masculine, creative, gallant, and rhythmical. Each dance of the tanda (the set of four tangos) and our cohesion improved. By the last turn of the last dance, I knew his embrace by heart. With a slight bow we both said *merci,* moved apart and then to opposite shores of the ballroom. I filed him away in my head; I had found another sleeper cell to dance with on another night, maybe at another place but we would discover each other again. I don't know his name; he didn't ask mine. So many years after my very first tango there are still these pearls that drop into my lap.

How do I love tango? Let me count the ways. I love tango like that soulmate myth – like the man I once loved and probably still do and like the man I will someday find and love who will love me back. In the meanwhile, I'm betrothed to tango.

There are many ways to be happy and life offers so very many passions to partake of. But there is something elemental about moving to music with others. It's in our DNA. So I suggest you take yourself to dance or wake up the reluctant spouse with your own overflow of energy. Register for salsa, ballroom, elementary ballet, intermediate jazz and modern or sink into Argentine tango. Find a bar with line dancing, a local Y that offers folk or a crash course in pre-wedding dance classes but just do it! Don't wait for the New Year because you'll change your mind by then as reality or something like it, will set in. Find a place that has a wood floor, mirrors, and lots of other people who glow with the secret that dancers, both amateur and pro, from five to ninety-five know: there's no faster way to find your spirit than on the dance floor. It's like crossing over into the eternal party room whether or not it's holiday season or there's any sort of occasion. It always feels like a celebration.

Please don't protest you have no sense of rhythm or have those proverbial two left feet; the dance world *specializes* in people with two left feet! Don't dismiss dance for skinny people or young people, musical or artistic people. Dance is for *human* people like you. Yes, *you* the one who dances around the kitchen, waiting for sugar cookies to cool. Yes, you who secretly want to make that Cinderella entrance to the ball. Don't wait for an invitation, just go! Slip into those glass slippers, pat down those wings so no one sees just how magic it all is and just how magical you can be.

If you're still waiting and debating about going to tango after all this, don't worry. Tango, bless its warm, Latin-fevered heart, will wait for you. *El tango te espera….* tango waits for you. I hope to see you one day soon and when I do I'll say, *Hola, would you like to dance*? I can promise you an unlimited adventure. It won't be *my* adventure; it will be *yours* and because of that it will be imperfectly perfect.

A BRIEF HISTORY OF TANGO

First, a caveat:
How Argentine Tango Differs from Ballroom Tango.

Argentine tango, versus *ballroom* tango is generally defined as a social dance as other dances are but Argentine tango is such a separate beast that grouping it alongside other dances is inadequate. Compared to almost all other social dances I've tried like ballroom as well as ballet, modern, jazz, folk and theatrical, *Argentine* tango is another universe entirely. It's also the tango we associate with the romantic mystique of the word *tango* and the subject of this book.

Argentine tango is a phenomenon of personal expression, one that's done to music, choreographed on the fly, in an ad-hoc partnership with another person who more often than not is a total stranger. Kindly don't confuse the tango I'm all lit up about with ballroom dance or ballroom-style or *Continental* style tango or *Dancing with the Stars.* They all feature tango but not the style of tango I'm talking about. So how is *Argentine* tango different from other types of tango?

For one thing, *Argentine* tango isn't heavily into world-wide competitions and dance contests nor does *Argentine* tango have 'levels' or other quantitative ways of judging the huge mainstream of tango dancers. To a significant extent, the traditional world of ballroom dance as well as *West Coast Swing, Swing, Salsa* and some other dance communities while mainly about the joy of social dance are also quite often about showmanship and performances which are rated. To that point, the other social dances and their communities, much like the figure skating circuit, offer many, world-wide competitive venues. Or drop into an Arthur Murray studio and they'll quickly explain the various levels you can aspire to.

In contrast, *Argentine* tango has *some* competitive venues but it's not the main game. Like all dance communities, tango does host conferences and festivals where dancers from other parts converge, learn and socialize. Another plus is that world-renown tango teachers come to teach at these events and the cross pollination of diverse people and visiting pros makes these exceptional events. That is just part of tango's wealth.

For many if not most other social dances, there is dance-style centric music they rely on for their dances. Folk dance has its tunes, as does Swing dance, cha-cha, salsa, merengue, etc. whereas tango (and West Coast swing) does have traditional tango dance music but you can also dance tango to pretty well sort of music and dance to either the rhythm or the melody line or interchangeably.

AND NOW, A BRIEF HISTORY OF TANGO

"I think those who say that you can't tango is you are not Argentinean are mistaken. Tango was immigrant music...so it does not have a nationality. It's only passport is a feeling"

Carlos Gavito

Say the word *tango* and the average person envisions a brooding male bending a woman dancer backwards in a dramatic pose. Or, perhaps it is that image of a woman, leaning on a man, her leg, sheathed in a skirt that is only as skin-tight as it is excessively slit up the side, writhing against the length of her partner's body. There's also the familiar image of a woman dancing with a red rose in her mouth a la *Carmen* in a dance and seduce tableau. But tango is so beyond these caricatures and so much more.

There are many tango websites that address the history of tango as well as books that attempt the same. Somehow few transmit the rich brocade of tango both the dance and its culture. For a dance that's a global passion spanning over 150 years ground-breaking books on tango are relatively few. To be honest, tango books, even as this one is, are uniquely centric as to the bias and background of the author. Still, I'm always surprised how difficult it seems to *simply tell* the story of the origin of tango and how it evolved. Understandably there's a lack of documentation in its very early days which are comparatively murkier than the last sixty years or so. It cannot be understated that tango history is not exactly a linear one and it's fraught with uprisings, revolutions and cultural impact. Some like to tout that at one point one pope or another banned tango but that's more an unsubstantiated legend than an historical fact and the reverse may be true. Tango as it now stands now and for a long time, is a globally-embraced dance that is the lifeblood of those that do it it's almost an international language as music is.

It's also a language that's keenly tethered to art, politics, culture, music, and film.

For something so popular, it's strange that Argentine Tango is shrouded in misinformation and divergent theories. That this is so in an age where the Internet's calling card is information-overload as well information being incredibly democratically accessible makes even less sense.

This is likely due to the fact that there is a dearth of material but it's in Spanish and not in English. Similarly, websites that are English-language based still only partially explain things and can be rife with misinformation or inaccuracies although everything is improving as tango gains popularity. This said one of the best blogs on tango that is in English is *Tango Voice* https://tangovoice.

wordpress.com/2022/09/14/a-framework-for-analyzing-the-evolution-of-tango-social-dancing/. It's somewhat academic in tone and no one seems to know its author but it does offer a lot of food for thought.

By comparison, the history of tango music is a bit more linear and different writers on the subject have a lot more congruency in their accounts. What's interesting here however is that there's a few hundred recognizable, classic or iconic tango tunes from prior decades, these days, with the advent of *Nuevo* tango, tango is danced to almost *any* sort of music, tango being very accommodating. The music doesn't have to be tango-centric in its roots or Argentinian-composed to do the trick. That said there's no mistaking the summoning to the dance floor that a di Sarli, d'Arieno, or Pugliese classic tune can evoke or the satisfying end of a great tango evening as the first chords of *La Comparisita* is played.

The tango evolved about 1880 in dance halls, coventillor (community housing) and perhaps brothels in the lower-class districts of Buenos Aires, where the Spanish tango, a light-spirited variety of flamenco, merged with the milonga campera (countryside), a fast, sensual, and disreputable Argentine dance; it also shows possible influences from the Cuban habanera as well as African rhythms. As time went on, milonga style tango and music split to distinctly tango and milonga.

Source: https://www.britannica.com

Tango: There is no agreement as to the etymology of this word. When it comes to the pre-history of tango everything is shrouded in a dense fog.

Source: www.totango.net

In Argentina, circa 1880 or so, there were once a lot of *gauchos* or what could be called South American cowboys. These were rustic, adventurous men – rebels of a sort -and they did folkish dances inspired by Africans and their own music/dance called the *habera.* Some sources say the dance or the music was called the *tambo* which segued to *tango.*

To further confuse things tango also had a faster, choppier version of itself called the *milonga. Milonga* actually means dance and in addition to being a faster paced tango milonga also refers to a 'dance evening'. So, you can *do* a milonga (faster tango dance) or *attend* a milonga or *do* a milonga *at* a milonga!! This makes total sense to tango people but if you are a newbie or outsider you would definitely find this a bit of a mix-up.

After the *gauchos* came their sons, the next generation, aka the *compadres.* The compradres further perfected the dance of tango and advanced it a great deal. Unlike the gauchos hero/rebel/loners, the *compradres* were far more diligent. The sons of the gauchos sons wandered less, got jobs in the cities, trained and learned city worker skills such as being butchers and salesmen and in a sense, they were the tango yuppies of Argentina.

At this point tango was often men dancing with men, dancing with and for each other as part of their practice. This also makes sense if you consider that at this point men in Argentina outnumbered women fifty to one and if you're a well-practiced leader, you'll have a better shot of dancing with the minority of women in attendance at a social dance function.

Then came the *compadres'* sons, the *Compadritos.* As with other generations that follow the ones that did more heavy lifting, this generation worked a bit less hard, having inherited more ease that comes with more material things and more daily life certainty. These were not rustic folk or rebels but a slicker working class. They danced tango in the streets to the bandoneon street players. These were also street shoe-shine boys who entertained customers while waiting for other customers and some of these also played tango music with the bandoneon, the boxy, accordion-like instrument that is tango's heritage voice. In addition to the compadres, there was significant immigration to Argentina in the mid/late 1800's to early 1900's, bringing with it European newcomers interested in developing culture and offering their own imprint on the music in particular as evidenced by the Italian names of tango composers in that time.

Although there's a lot of unsubstantiated lore or legends of men dancing with men, while waiting for their bordello 'dates', it seems more historically correct that dancing took place in modest dance halls. The political class at the time frowned on the passionate dancing apparently but there isn't much to suggest repression or laws against it. But that tale of bordello/tango origins has long put a taint or discredited the history of tango and make it marginal. As the interest in tango became mainstream and other classes adopted it, the politicos accepted it more and the dance segued to better dance venues.

The Golden Age of Tango

From rebel gauchos to dancing in bordellos - tango maintained its street/low-life, rebel/loner mentality. It was quite populist and when the Argentinean revolution came, tango, associated with a rebel as well as a lower class sensibility was suppressed and frowned on and held on by a thread. But then Argentineans started travelling. In Paris, in particular, there were travelling Argentineans. Although they could not at this time tango in their Argentinean homeland in Paris tango took on a new élan and enjoyed a positive reception. This occurred about around 1920 thru the 1930's and 40's and Europeans were enthralled. Paris may have helped establish tango's growing cachet it but you cannot take the counter culture stitches out of the integral tango fabric which has an immutable Argentinean DNA. So when tango returned to its birth place, it came home to a post-revolutionary Argentina. There was freedom once again and the dance blossomed even more. It no longer had to hide or be otherwise banned as the music and dance of 'immoral societal elements'.

In the 30's, 40's and 50's tango entered what is now referred to as its 'golden age' and it was embraced, blossomed and evolved. The ballrooms, cafes and streets overflowed with tango-loving citizens. But then in the 60's, the flower-hippie filled 60's, worldwide life was changing.

In concert with this change, music and dance began to evolve and Buenos Aires born Astor Pizzazolla came around along with his music, around 1948-1980. Here was a native son of Argentina who was a composer like none other. He totally deconstructed and broadened tango music incredibly and pivoted forward in a quantum leap.

Pizzazolla was credited with a totally new music called *Nuevo tango* that was dramatic, rhythmical, captivating and bold. He also spent a lot of time in New York and had much collaboration with jazz musicians which resulted in beautiful musical cross pollination of jazz and tango. But many felt (Astor himself) that his music wasn't really traditional tango music for dancers; it was more tango music for listeners. It also caused old time tango devotees, purists, and the traditional tango establishment to reject him. He was loved and hated throughout his professional career for both rejuvenating and betraying tango.

But Pizzazollo's sound might have ignited more than just a break with tradition. Perhaps people weren't embracing his music as danceable or traditional but it did bring a lot of new attention to tango itself. In the late 80's, early nineties, once again tango bloomed and became a world-wide phenomenon. It had its second golden age around the mid-to-late 80's to late 90's as people brought tango home from trips to Buenos Aires and tango teachers set up studios and began to spread to word. It is exactly around this time that I discovered tango and the energy in those days was palatable and addictive. Anyone who started then remembers it in a special, once-in-a-life-time way. I just happen to be one of them who stayed and found more special times ever after.

Tango music is evolving exponentially, both in terms of polished, rescued recordings of the classic music but also with new tango musicians and composers. I would say, pandemics notwithstanding, tango in the 21st Century is going well. Overall, there are more people dancing tango and tango continues to be cross cultural as well as cross generational – two things which ensure the continuance of its longevity. That's another thing about tango: other dances are more rigorous or can be. With tango, you can be energized or simply walk slowly and rhythmically which makes it a go-the-distance dance, as evidenced as the many dancers in their 80's and beyond. You don't have to age out in tango. Tango, as all dance does, offers a lot of sheer joy, especially if you dance the fast paced milonga or a waltz tango but it is the slower-metered classic songs that reveals the darker underbelly of its roots. There's always the romance in tango music but it comes with that vibe of something a bit underground, steamy and soulful and I think that is what makes it addictive in part, as well as the fact you get to meet in this sad, musical place with another person and express it together, Alternatively, you can focus on the technique and music and it's elements of a pure social dance and enjoy it from that perspective too.

The history of tango is one that wends this way and that and it takes a lot of reading and research to really pin down all its sketchy places. Moreover, those that know it best, that older generation who came of age in tango's first golden era, is now slipping away. Those who love the history of the dance as well as participate in it are left to piece it together, adding pieces of fabric, like décor on a tango dance itself, as it goes along.

Sometimes people consider tango to be Argentina's gift to the world since tango can be found all over the globe. But if you consider that the roots of tango come from Europe and Africa but someone rooted better in Argentina and came of age there, that's rather interesting. It reminds me of the Scots who brought their wheat seeds from their native land to Canada and discovered that their beautiful red wheat grew better on the Canadian prairies than their homeland. Somehow, Argentina was the germination dance floor as it were, and tango came of age there. I still also find that when I dance with someone from Argentina they dance with the confidence of the 'manner born'. It's just in their genes.

Like the Argentinean cowboys who began it, tango never lost its rebel heritage, whether you do it in the streets of Buenos Aires, dressed up in a swanky hotel ballroom in Helsinki, in distressed jeans in the hillsides of Vermont or in a vintage dress in a park in

Montreal. You're as entitled to tango as anyone else. Think of tango as its own nation with its own language. It's a place where the only passport is essentially just knowing how to walk to music which is something anyone can do. I suggest you learn tango and obtain your tango passport so you can visit tango anywhere you go in the world or just at your local community center. Tango makes you feel at home no matter where you are.

And once you know a little tango, then when someone asks you to dance, you'll know they're not just saying: *would you like to dance?* They're really saying: *Do you speak tango?* Count yourself lucky and be very glad if you can answer *yes* because they're not just asking you to step onto a dance floor, they are inviting you to the world. They're inviting you into life.

SPECIAL ACKNOWLEDGMENTS

Thank you to Tomás Howlin

The History of Tango section was assisted by the expertise and generous editorial input of Tomás Howlin, a globe-trotting tango teacher, historian and performer. You can read more about Tomás here https://www.tomastango.com/bio.

Thank you to the Montreal tango studios, venues and tango hosts of the parks of the city -

In particular, and with much affection and respect to Carol Horowitz and Studio Tango, Tango Libre, Mon Tango, La Tangueria, Las Piernas Tango, West Island Tango, Cozy Tango, Tango Club Rive-Nord, Café Moka, and the dearly departed Tango Fabrika and Graffiti Tango

If you've enjoyed this book, I hope to see you at tango one day soon! In the meanwhile, you can also visit me at my cookbook author, baking site, www.betterbaking.com where you'll find my recipe for **Tango Cookies** and so much more as well as links to all my many cookbooks as well as one book of poetry, *Love and Ordinary Things.*

Made in the USA
Middletown, DE
26 August 2023

37118430R00136